The Beggar

Table of contents

Chapter 1

I Am Sam King

My name is Sam King. I'm twenty-one years old, living in downtown Detroit and I'm a trash collector. A member of Detroit's "Advanced Disposal Team" if you want to get into specific role titles. Not the most glamorous job, having to run behind a garbage truck loading and unloading street after street of haphazardly placed bins left almost mindlessly out for collection. Not the most mentally stimulating job by any stretch of the imagination either. And definitely not a job for the squeamish, given some of the revolting smells and sights I've endured since I became part of the game. But someone has to do it. It's not a great paying job either, but it's enough to put food on the table and provide a roof over my head during these fierce Michigan winters.

I can't really say that I enjoy collecting the waste of the masses... in fact, I hate it. The job seriously trashes my self-esteem (pun intended), but, for now, I have no choice, as times are tough, and jobs are hard to find anywhere, let alone in downtown Detroit. I may hate my job, but I can't be too fussy about what I do. Despite it all—the crappy pay, the early mornings, the stigma, and the stench!—I guess I do consider myself lucky to have a job at all, even if it does leave my pride down in the gutter.

Life to me feels like a slog. It's working to pay for my existence and that's it; there's nothing left after I pay my bills and buy my food. Some days—most days—I feel born into slavery, as if I came here to just make someone else rich and end up with nothing in my pocket to show for my hard work. The possibility of creating some sort of life for myself and advance into doing what I really want to do seems so far out of reach.

I always dreamt of owning my own restaurant, one that would be affordable to anyone, rich or poor. Having grown up in poverty, we never had the luxury of going out as a family to eat in a nice restaurant (not some greasy fast-food joint). It was considered unaffordable to my parents, and, as with many families around us, money was always an issue. So, creating a place that gave less fortunate people a chance to enjoy the same experience as the more wealthy members of the community was an idea that really drove me. Albeit, executing it was far reaching and, for now, my dream stayed just that, a dream. There's something freeing about being your own boss. The thought of not having to answer to anyone, making my own decisions, working my own hours, and using my own imagination, without someone trying to squash it… is something that appeals to me, because I like to think that I'm a far more intelligent and creative man than your average garbage collector, working a mindless monotonous job like I do now. But despite how capable I might feel at times, my restaurant remains a pipe dream. I have to keep on with my

2

current job, and keep dreaming about owning my own restaurant one day.

I start work at five o'clock in the morning, and every morning it's the same old routine: bashing the alarm clock as it sounds; dragging myself out of bed, feeling depressed and unmotivated; and muttering, "I am so sick of this life!" Not exactly the most motivating mantra, I admit, but I'm truly sick of living hand to mouth, making a living collecting and disposing all the rejected foods and the wasted unnecessary things this city has to offer up daily.

People always tell me to be positive, think positive, stay positive! Yeah. Sure…. Easier said than done, especially when you live in a nice home instead of my ghetto apartment, which was an upgrade from a spot under a bridge. I'm not going to embrace this Pollyannaish "positive" fluff, and pretend to be happy when I live this life of struggle and drudgery. I work in garbage for Christ's sake! And my dream business is nowhere close to becoming a reality. What's to be glad or positive about? It's not like I've had a winning run so far, and now I've just hit the doldrums….My life feels like it has been a series of traumatic disappointments and challenges since childhood. The ability to be "positive" about my past is beyond me. I'm the type of person who likes to call it the way it is; I'm not going to pretend that garbage doesn't stink.

I grew up an only child in a modest home in Detroit. Detroit used to be a nice place to live, but over the years, it's become a dangerous and unpleasant place, full of crime and poverty. Nevertheless, I still love Detroit. It's where I was born, and I'll always feel a connection to this place.

My mother left us without warning when I was ten. She disappeared in the middle of the night, with only a few of her things and never came back. I remember that morning as if it were yesterday. I walked out of my room and went into the kitchen as I always did, expecting to see my Mom preparing some breakfast for us, as she normally did, but she wasn't there. The kitchen light was off, and all the pots and pans were still hanging on the rack above the stove. I thought she must've been still asleep, which was unusual, as she was always the first one to get up, but she wasn't in her bed either. I vividly remember calling out for her, looking for her, but she didn't answer... The house was filled with a deafening silence. I walked outside, and there was my father, sitting on the porch, rocking in his favorite chair, staring straight ahead, his eyes glazed.

"Where's Mom?" I asked my father. As he turned his head slowly toward me, the glaze of his sad eyes spilling into tears that dripped unhindered down his face. He grabbed me, held me close to him, and stroked my head with such a tender caress.

"Mom's gone, Son," he said slowly and clearly, although through a faltering voice.

I remember feeling the blood rush through my body. I couldn't understand what it meant. Confusion came quickly. I thought she had "gone" to the store, so I asked my father when she would be back from the store. His strength gave way and he burst out crying.

"No, Son, Mom's left... and she's... not coming back," he choked out between his wailing.

I'll never forget that day. I'll never forget the feeling I had when he said that. It seemed like everything was moving slowly around me.

There was a silence in my head, like time had stopped and I was waiting to wake up from a nightmare, and craving that sense of relief that this was only a horrific dream or a terrible joke... But I soon realized that there was no waking from this dream, that these events had indeed just played out, happening in my waking hours. This was our reality. From that day on, it was just my father and me. Both of us struggled to come to terms with my mother leaving. I remember asking a lot of questions, but my father couldn't give me any answers.

Years passed by.... I was fifteen when my father suffered a stroke. I remember the doctor telling him that it was due to excess stress and overwork. The stroke left him with a mildly significant paralysis on the left side of his body, rendering him unfit and able to drive; he had to leave his job as a truck driver. This, in turn, forced me to leave school and work to help support both myself and my father, who needed additional care and was dependant on regular medications that weren't cheap.

I managed to find a job as a janitor at a textile factory downtown. Luckily, I didn't look my age, "fudged" my date of birth on the application, and was hired. It was a small wage and, combined with my father's pension, just enough to support us. Despite securing work, the financial struggle continued, becoming harder and harder to get to the end of the month, without accruing some form of debt. Initially, my father was functioning reasonably well. But his condition deteriorated over time and he became less and less capable of even the simplest of tasks. This made him depressed, and affected his moods deeply, to the point where he would often sit on the porch for hours at a time and, without a word, stare with a cold straight face into what seemed like nothingness... As time went by, the level of special care my father needed increased significantly, and in order to cover these costs, he unfortunately had to remortgage the family home. This was another massive blow. Our house was our safety net, and to remortgage it, meant a high risk of losing the house, as we couldn't afford higher repayments. It was blow after blow after blow, and there I was, trying to make sense of it all, and hold it all together. Just like Dad had done all those years ago.

My father was a man who didn't show a lot of emotion. I remember being shocked when I saw him cry after my mother left, but he never spoke of his pain or how he felt. Despite that, I could see the anguish in his eyes. His eyes were always expressionless yet spoke of such a depth of pain and suffering. He spoke slowly and quietly, and always tried to do things by himself, without asking me for help. Sometimes, he would be in so much pain just trying to get out of his chair, but he wouldn't let me help him. He was a proud man, the "old school" type. I knew that he felt that he was a burden on me. I would often tell him how much I loved him, and that he was still useful and important, that I couldn't do it on my own, and that I needed him despite him feeling he was a burden.

The only "me" time I had was when I'd go to the local YMCA gym for a workout. It would help me get my mind off the problems at home and clear my head a little. It also helped me control and process my anger, which was growing as time went by. My current responsibilities were way above and beyond the scope of any fifteen-year-old by a long shot, and my time at the gym gave me great motivation and strength, both physically and mentally. I grew to become very fit, strong, and muscular after spending so much time at the gym over the next few years of my life. This was no disadvantage for someone who's living in the slums of downtown Detroit.....to look a little intimidating isn't such bad thing.

Shortly after I turned eighteen, my father died following another massive stroke, leaving me both an empty, aching heart and a mountain of health bills that had been accumulated during my father's treatment. Consequently, I was forced to relinquish the family home to pay for the debt. To add to my agony, the textile factory I had been working in closed down due to a fire, leaving me homeless and unemployed on the streets of Detroit, distraught with grief over the loss of my father, and with no money and very little possessions.

For the next few weeks after my father's death and losing everything, I lived in a shelter in downtown Detroit and sometimes under the Detroit Bridge when the shelter was at its full capacity. I was always in survival mode. I would collect aluminium cans and glass bottles and sell them at the collection depot for a few dollars. I used to see that on TV and movies, where homeless people collected cans and wheeled them around in shopping carts, so I thought that was what I should do also. That enabled me to buy some basic groceries for the week and keep them in my bag. Sometimes, this method of earning money didn't work out, as finding cans and bottles proved hard at times, so stealing food in order to eat was my other option I resorted to. This was basically my routine to stay alive, and, in between, I'd look for whatever job I could find.

This was also significantly challenging. Times were tough, and for every job vacancy, there were hundreds of applicants, so the competition was fierce. I applied for all sorts of jobs, but every time, I was told the same thing; I wasn't qualified enough, or they had chosen someone who's more suited.
Leaving school at a young age to work as a janitor wasn't exactly the qualification or "job history" they were looking for.

One afternoon, after collecting a bag full of aluminium cans, I went to the depot to sell the cans. It must have been my lucky day because the manager of the recycling depot noticed me and my particularly large physique as it later turned out. He approached me with a steady and purposeful swagger.

"Hey there, brother! You seem mighty strong for a can collector... With muscles like that, you could probably do something a bit more 'pay worthy,'" he said, nodding toward my upper body. He held my gaze and winked as he said, "worthy." "What's your name, brother?"

"Sam..." I said slowly. "What do you have in mind?" I asked, eying him suspiciously while unloading the cans from my bag.

"Well!" he said, "with your size and strength, we could definitely use you on our garbage collection runs. It's not an executive job, and it's only five hours a day five days a week, but it pays far better than what the cans business will make you," he chuckled kindly. "You look pretty fit... Bet you can easily handle the pace of the truck, and it's obvious that you have the strength to empty out the bins on the domestic runs."

At this point, I was willing to do anything. I was so desperate to put an end to my homelessness and have a comfortable place to live in. A smile crept to my lips.... I allowed it to spread across my face. I looked him in the eyes; he returned the look with strength and encouragement as I started nodding.

"Sure! I'll take it! When do I start!?" I replied with an eager enthusiasm.

"You can start tomorrow. Be here at 5 a.m. sharp, you can team up with Joshua, one of our veteran guys; he'll show you the ropes."

"Thank you, sir! I really appreciate it!" I replied excitedly.

"Call me Mark," he said and shook my hand. "I'll see you then, Sam."

And that was the pivotal beginning of my career with Detroit's Advanced Waste Disposal team....

That day, the shelter reached full capacity by 4 p.m., but I didn't care. I was elated by my chance meeting with Mark at the depot! I went to my usual spot under the bridge, feeling a massive sense of relief that I now had paying job that would enable me to secure a place to live and get my life back in order. I gazed at the stars, and spoke to my father. I told him I had gotten a job and that I was okay. As a young boy, I always believed that when you die, you become a star in the sky. So now that my father had joined the ranks of divine stars, I would often look up at the starry skies and talk to my Dad.... believing, knowing that he could hear me.

Within a week of starting my new job, I moved into a small apartment. It wasn't very fancy. In fact, it was a derelict building, but it was what I could afford, and I was so happy just be off the streets. I also made a friend. Joshua, my fellow garbage collector. Joshua and I hit it off from the very first day. I think I look up to him as sort of a father figure, and his sunny attitude is a refreshing break from my gloomy thoughts, even if I do disagree with him most of the time.

Three years later, I was still working with Joshua and wondering why. Even Joshua was wondering why. "When are you going to quit and start your restaurant business?" Joshua asked one morning as he dumped a bin from a restaurant into the truck. "Wouldn't you rather be serving people sweet-smelling food instead of dumping their stinking rotten food?"

"All I need is a winning lottery ticket," I replied. "Can't save any money working this job. Christ, I can barely make enough to pay rent and utilities. To tell you the truth, Josh, I never imagined that this garbage-collecting job would be a long-term thing. I always imagined myself working hard, saving hard, living frugally, and making enough money to start my own restaurant."

"You're still young yet. Things will change and you'll get your break. You might not win the lottery, but you you're smart; you don't need luck."

"Yeah, thing will change alright, for the worse," I countered. "The economy isn't in very good shape. People are being laid off and I don't think there's much chance of my becoming self-employed any time soon."

"Well, at least you got a steady job."

"Oh yeah? Even that's doubtful for long. I heard a rumor that a cutback in the budget could mean some men may be laid off, Whenever I turn up for work, I feel relieved when I'm handed a worksheet instead of getting the sack. I don't want to move back to my old digs under the bridge. I tell you, Josh, I worry so much; I have trouble sleeping at night."

"That's your problem, Sam; you worry too much. It don't do any good to worry. It's not going to change the future; it'll just make you feel bad. So why not hope for the best? Long ago, before my experience, I was just as stubborn, fearful, and insecure. But I found my bliss and peace within myself, and now I'm happy with my life, working two jobs to support my family."

"You never told me what that experience was, Josh. You gonna tell me now?"

"Uh-uh. It's not something you talk about in between emptying garbage bins!" shouted Joshua over the roar of the truck engine.

"Maybe during break, then," I suggested as we arrived back at the depot for our midmorning break.

After getting our coffees and sitting down, Joshua said, "I don't know if you're ready to hear it, Sam. Heck, you don't even listen when I tell you how a positive attitude can turn your life from drudgery to bliss."

"What's so goddamn blissful about my mother leaving me, huh?!" I demanded across the break room table.

Joshua smiled kindly. "There's always a reason for everything, and, sometimes, the reason becomes apparent after we accumulate enough life experience," he then continued with his spiritual indoctrination… "The Universe knows you, Sam, and it has a perfect plan for you."

"Yeah right! Blah, blah… blah," I answered with scorn in my voice. "It has a plan for me?! This Universe of yours….took away my mother, killed my father, and left me all alone and scared under a bridge with nothing. If this is the best plan your Universe can come up with for me, then it better go back to the drawing board! Give me a break, Josh!"

"Well, enough about that," said Joshua, changing the subject. "You gonna see Selena tonight?"

"As per usual. I'm surprised I haven't developed an allergy to chocolate after all the chocolate milkshakes I've had. And I don't even like them."

Joshua laughed. "Well, you'll just have to ask her out, so you won't need a milkshake as an excuse to see her. You're a handsome guy, Sam. I bet she'd love to go out with you.

"C'mon, Josh. Face it; handsome or not, I'm living in a dump, working with a dump, and can hardly afford to pay for a date, much less gather the courage to tell Selena where I live or what I do, questions that will most certainly come up very early in the conversation. I'm just not ready for it."

For months now, I've had a crush on Selena, the waitress at Frank's Diner. She doesn't know it, and I have no intention of telling her, of course, but it's nice to fantasize sometimes. From the day I first laid eyes on her, I was mesmerized. Enthralled. I even ordered a second milkshake that first time at the diner, just so I could drink in her magnificent beauty while I ingested my chocolate-laden excuse to stay. I told her I was a student and that I lived with my parents. It felt guilty to lie like that, but I just couldn't stand feeling the embarrassment of her knowing what I did and where I lived.

In the absence of any relationships, both the friendly and intimate variety, I try to do things that elevate my mind. One of my most enjoyable activities is taking long walks by the Detroit River. Every day after work, I walk along the water, allowing my mind to wander freely. It's my time of peace and contemplation. It's a time when I

12

often dream of the things and circumstances that would make my ideal life a complete reality.

Today after work, my eyes were drawn to a park bench along the walking path, emblazoned with an advertisement for an old lottery jackpot. I fantasized about what I would do if I won millions of dollars. I thought about how great it would be to be free from worrying about money again, and how that would improve my insecurities. I thought how great it would be to be able to pay my bills easily and without having to ask for extensions. To have my own place and not have to beg the landlord for more time to pay, which is so demoralizing, and is hardest thing to do, since my landlord is an old tightwad with not much sympathy for anything. He's so tight that, sometimes, I can hear a squeak from his butt cheeks when he walks; so, to ask for rent extension, or anything to do with credit, requires a lot of practice and expertise in the field of the dramatic arts in order to touch his heart and induce sympathy.

I also thought about how great it would be to have friends and not have to hide my life of poverty from them. To actually be somebody. Since I didn't have much of a childhood, hence no childhood friends, I often wondered if my life would have turned out differently had I stayed in school and managed to grow up in some form of normalcy. How awesome it would be to have a girlfriend without fear of having to disclose my life of poverty to her. I honestly believe that money would solve all my problems. I truly believe that the reason I have no one to love and no friends, is because I'm a poor garbage man and with nothing much to offer.

People will continue to parrot off the old nugget that "Money can't buy happiness," yet I feel everything that's happened in my life so far wouldn't have happened if I'd had money or would have turned out

13

for the better if money hadn't been so scarce. My father would have been alive, we would never have lost the house, and I would never have worked with garbage. So maybe they don't need money for happiness, but I sure as hell do.

On impulse, and with money on my mind, I decided to go to Remi's corner store not far from where I live and buy a lottery ticket. I guess that advertisement inspired me. Remi is your classic Jamaican man. His exceptionally long dreadlocks cover his back, a knitted cap covers his head, and a smile as wide as the Grand Canyon fills his face. I'd routinely find him arguing boisterously about a recent soccer game with random customers. It's a real comedy show, listening to all of them give their interpretation of the game, their loud and passionate accents competing to be heard over the next. You'd better not interrupt, even if you wanted to purchase something.

As I entered the corner shop, Remi, sure enough, was complaining about the game last night with his Jamaican friends.

"Jero should have come from the left!"

"He shoulda passed it to Bega!"

Further disagreement. "No way, maan; Jero was in di right posishon!" So it would go all day, providing Remi had a ready and willing customer or friend to analyze a recent match.

"Morning Remi," I greeted. Remi was still in the middle of his passionate analysis of poor old Jero's performance, so I had to just stand there and wait. It wasn't long before Remi stopped talking and turned his head toward me.

14

"Yo, Sammy! How's it hang'n, maan!" he greeted me with his croaky voice. "What do you think Jero should have done, huh?!" he asked, still all revved up.

"Sorry, Remi, I don't watch soccer…." I laughed.

"So you're here for a lottery ticket?" he chuckled and winked. "Ready for the jackpot?! It's thirty million big ones this week, maan!" he exclaimed excitedly in his rich Jamaican accent. Remi has sold me many tickets before. He knows very well how much I'm dreaming about winning the lottery.

"Yep!" I said. "Gotta be in it to win it, brother! And make sure it's a winning one this time! No more crappy nonwinning tickets!" I laughed.

With a Tai Chi "turn and chop," Remi murmured an Asian-sounding prayer as if he were a Tibetan monk, hit the print button of the lotto ticketing machine, and handed it to me, singing, "Kumbaya, my Lotto, Kumbaya! I feel that's a winner, Sammy boy." He laughed again.

"From your mouth to God's ears," I replied. "Thanks Remi! You crazy cat!"

I chuckled and left the corner shop, toward Frank's Diner for my favorite milkshake and to hopefully catch a glimpse of my favorite waitress, Selena. Damn! No matter how I'm feeling on any particular day, I'm guaranteed to lose my nerves as soon as I lay eyes on her. I'm like a high school boy who has a crush on his teacher. Selena is a young university premed student, something I'm significantly intimidated by because, when I think about it, it's not exactly an even

15

playing field. "Premed Student" versus "garbage man." This comparison in career achievement status most definitely doesn't help my confidence.

Selena owns the world's most beautiful smile, a smile that quite often makes me weak in the knees and breathless simultaneously. I've always been in awe of her beauty, and when she speaks to me, I'm rendered speechless. She has this really cute lisp, more so when she says my name. Her hair is always tied up in a ponytail that flips from shoulder to shoulder whenever she moves her head when she's speaking. The combination of her lisp, the movement of her ponytail, her smile, and her vivacious voice is a little too much for my nerves. Any sense of calm or ease dissipates as soon as I see her gorgeous face, and all I can think about is how utterly amazing she is.

I entered the diner and sat in my usual booth next to the window. She walked up to me with a huge smile on her face, like I was the best thing that entered the diner since Santa Claus.

"Hi, Tham," Selena greeted me with her cute lisp and a shining smile that would make any man's jaw drop. "The usual?"

"Yes please, Selena," I replied with a shy voice.

Selena brought the milkshake to my table. "How was your day?" she asked with interest that was obviously genuine.

"Pretty m..m..monotonous," I replied with a tired, broken voice. "How are your studies going?" I asked.

"Well, two more years to go, but it's getting more and more challenging. Hopefully, it'll all be worth it....I'm not intending on being a waitress for the rest of my life you know!" She laughed her adorable laugh; it reminded me of a soft melodic song.

Oh my God! That laugh! I thought as I slurped my milkshake. We chatted for a few more minutes, until a customer tried to get Selena's attention.

"I'll be one minute," she said cheerfully to the lady waiting. She turned back to me and said, "Good to see you today, Tham…"

"Well, I better get going. I'll be missing you when you're gone."

"Well I'm not going yet." She laughed again and her eyes twinkled brightly, accenting her song-like laughter.

"Good to hear… See you soon," I said and walked toward the front door.

"Bye, Tham," she said with a sweet voice and what seemed like a look of admiration in her eyes.

I always get the urge to look back at Selena through the window when I leave the diner. It's like I want to test her to see if she'd give me another look, and she often does along with a wave goodbye. This simple exchange through the glass makes my heart soar.

I want to ask her out on a date, but I always hold back with the assumption that a woman who studies to become a doctor, possessing such beauty and intelligence as Selena does, would never be interested in a poor garbage collector. I'm sure she has a lot of admirers, far more well off and inspiring than me. If I were honest with myself, this assumption is just an excuse to avoid approaching

17

her, because deep down I feel like a loser for not being able to garner the courage. The assumption that she must have other admirers, further deflates my ego, and convinces me that there's a good reason, beyond my insecurities, why I don't ask her out.

My self-esteem has sunk to such a low level, that it's easier to create a routine for myself and hide inside my shell rather than put myself through the emotional turmoil and risk of rejection that seems to be attached with forging close relationships. So, I stay in my routine existence: rising early for a job that I dread, to pay for an apartment that I feel ashamed of. My highlights—the saving graces that give me small bursts of energy, positivity and light—are long walks and spending those blissful moments at the diner with the enchanting Selena....

Chapter 2

Meeting the Beggar

The day I met the beggar was a cold, spring day. The weather matched my mood because I had finally decided to end it all. I would go to my doctor and get a prescription for sleeping pills. I had some left over from a previous prescription. Then I would take both bottles and go to sleep for a very long time. I had just clocked off from my shift at the depot and decided to take one last walk along the Detroit River, down to Elizabeth Park. I often would sit on a park bench, admiring the views of Windsor, the Canadian side of the river. I loved spotting the people walking along the opposite side of the water. I would sometimes wave at them and wonder whether they were happier over there... on the other side. I wondered if I would be happy on the other side of life.

The sunlight glistened upon the water, broken into thousands of shining diamonds that flickered over the ripples created by the wind as it blew lightly across the water. I love this image of natural magic, so majestic and special, a never-ending flow of reflection, for as long as there was sun to shine light.

For some reason, I wasn't in my usual contemplative state of deep thinking from a place of darkness and lack. I was experiencing what you might call a feeling of hope and light heartedness. An auspicious feeling. I couldn't pinpoint exactly what it was or what caused it. Perhaps my decision to end my suffering was a relief. All I knew was that I felt as if something had erased my depression and worries for the afternoon. The previous night had been tough, a long, hard night sobbing myself to sleep, feeling hopeless and scared, but I suddenly felt all of those feelings being lifted away and a sense of divine presence taking over me... lifting a veil of fear and hopelessness, allowing me to see things differently.

As I stood there by the water, mesmerized by the sun's rays dancing across the surface, diamond reflections flickering and emanating golden rippling circles that slowly faded into nothingness, I heard a voice next to me.

"Don't worry about your life, son; you're exactly where you're supposed to be...."

I looked around, startled, to where the voice was coming from. On the ground, on top of a scrappy piece of old cardboard, sat a man, wearing a tattered and worn black coat, sporting a long gray beard and a shock of untamed frizzy hair. I immediately thought to myself, *This man is in dire need of a shower.*

"Excuse me?!" I demanded incredulously. "Were you talking to me?!"

The man looked at me with smiling eyes and slowly nodded back at me in approval.

"Did you just say, 'Don't worry; I'm exactly where I'm supposed to be?!'" I asked, without attempting to hide my annoyance.

The man nodded again, looking deeply into my eyes. "Do you have a light?" he asked with a cheeky grin while pointing a half-smoked cigarette at me.

"No, sorry, I don't smoke," I said and started to walk away from the man. Something made me stop, turn around, and walk back to the man, and, with a raised eyebrow and a look of curiosity on my face, I asked. "Why did you say I'm exactly where I need to be? How would you know where I am or where I need to be? By the looks of it, you'd better worry about whether YOU are where you need to be because, from where I'm standing, it doesn't look like you're in a position to give advice to anyone."

The man smiled again. A calm and peaceful smile.

"You're probably right if you judge me by appearance. But I used to be where you are.... and I know exactly where you're going. Yes, I may be poor, and I don't have a lot of possessions, but I sleep well at night and my soul is at peace... Is your soul at peace, Sam?" he asked slowly and deliberately, his deep blue eyes piercing mine in both a questioning and confronting way.

At that moment, I felt the hairs on the back of my neck bristle. "How the hell do you know my name?!" I demanded with a slight level of aggression in my voice. "Do I know you?!" I was troubled and perplexed that this random bum knew my name and possessed such audacity to question my happiness.

The man cast his eyes down to the ground, straightening his half-smoked cigarette.

"I see you walking here every day. You always look troubled.... and sad." The beggar said to me softly.

I felt my annoyance growing in reaction to this stranger judging me like that.

"That doesn't explain how you knew my name!" I retorted obnoxiously, still not sure what to make of this man and his purported knowledge. "Sometimes, I see the same people when I walk here, but their names don't just pop into my head. How did you know my name?!" I persisted. No response.

"Who are you?!" I asked again, with increased irritation in my voice.

The man raised his head slowly toward me, looking straight into my eyes.

"I know who I am; do you know who you are, Sam?" he asked.

"This is bullshit!" I retorted, my anger, frustration, and confusion equally clouding my brain.

A middle-aged man jogged past, slowing down and looking at me strangely with his face scrunched up, like he was looking at a crazy person. The man passed me and, after a few feet, turned his head back toward me and gave me another look as if I were a ghost.

22

"What are you looking at?!" I called to the jogger, my voice filled with exasperation. The jogger shook his head and increased his pace, moving away from me quickly, as if his life were in danger.

"What the hell is going on here?!" I yelled with utter frustration up into the bright afternoon sky. I felt rocked to the core and downright confused that this stranger, this bum knew my name and had the gall to judge me.

"Do you have a couple of spare dollars son?" the beggar asked with a cheeky grin on his face.

"No, I don't!" I replied impatiently. "Now, will you please tell me... how do you know my name?!" I asked again, demanding an answer with intensity blazing in both my words and my eyes.

"I know a lot about you, Sam," the man spoke again cryptically, quietly.

I couldn't believe what I was hearing.

"You know a lot about me?!? This is insane! How can you know anything about me? I've never even met you before today..."

The man smiled at me again with a compassionate look in his eyes.

"You can know a lot about someone just by observing them. Did you know that?" he said with a cocky, yet tongue-in-cheek tone. "The way they walk. The way they talk, and carry themselves. All the way through to the not so obvious things...their expressions and their energy. In fact, if you're in tune, you won't even have to meet them in order to know them...." He laughed gently, a laugh that reminded me of Joshua and his hearty, love-filled laugh.

"Energy?! Whatever, man!" I replied with apparent scorn in my voice and I shook my head in disapproval, thinking to myself this man was definitely crazy.

"We all have an energy field surrounding us," explained the man. "It's called an aura. It's like a magnetic field surrounding you, and that field sends out information about you." The man continued, "Have you ever stood next to a person you didn't know but felt that something was 'off' about them?"

"You mean like what I'm feeling toward you right now? Yeah, many times!" I smirked.

The man laughed at my remark. "Well, this is your unmatched auras clashing; this energy field can and will attract and repel people from you, depending on what's going on inside both you and them."

I was intrigued, but also unconvinced... and confused. The notion of a person's energy having cause and effect on another person by way of information sent through magnetic fields was something I'd never contemplated. It sounded so bizarre. Yet something deep within me was urging me to listen to this crazy beggar and his theories on observation and energy fields.

"So you just sat there, observing me and my energy... and now you claim to know me? And that I'm where I'm supposed to be? Not to mention my name?!" I was desperate for an explanation for this. "How did you know my name? From observation?!"

24

My need for a logical explanation was becoming apparent; I clutched at straws to make sense of this exchange. "I bet Joe told you my name!" I almost shouted, pointing at the hotdog vendor on the corner.

The man laughed, obviously amused by my reactions. "Do I scare you, Sam?" he asked softly.

"No you don't scare me!" I scoffed. "And I don't have time for this crap from a man who begs for money instead of earning it!"

The man laughed again, gently. "From a materialistic point of view, I am what you see on the surface: an old, poor human. But from a holistic point of view, I am what's inside of me: abundance and wisdom...."

"You're full of it; that's what inside of you!" I countered. "I'm out of here!" I declared abruptly and started to walk away from this deluded old beggar.

A woman pushing a baby carriage noticed my little tantrum and gave me the same kind of look the jogger had given me minutes earlier, a look of equal parts fear, concern, astonishment, and perplexity.

I held her eye contact and demanded in an angry voice, "What?!"

I turned back to the beggar and asked in a grumbling voice, "Why is everybody looking at me like I just landed from another planet?!"

The beggar laughed a big belly laugh, which didn't help the anger and confusion I was processing.

"No, Sam, they're not looking at you as if you're an alien; they're looking at you because they think you're crazy for talking to me!" He started to chuckle again.

"Yeah! They're probably right," I said.

By this point, I wasn't too amused with this strange encounter. All I had wanted was to take a walk along my favorite river, as I always do, and not be confronted with judgement or probed with philosophical questions by a beggar who appeared out of nowhere, claiming to know me, who I am, and where I need to be. I needed some space.

"Have a nice life!" I wished upon the man and walked away feeling uneasy.

As much as I needed to remove myself from this conversation, I was quite intrigued by the beggar. It was a bizarre discourse, and as crazy as he sounded, my meeting with the old man and the things he said had resonated within me. I couldn't stop wondering how he knew my name, and why he said he knew where I was supposed to be.

The man was a beggar, but he didn't come across as someone down on his luck. Yes, he was wearing filthy old clothes, smeared with the dirt of life and obviously homeless, yet he wasn't your average "beggar." He seemed quite intelligent. He was grounded, although not too serious. He had a very calm disposition and manner. He was easygoing and didn't seem worried about much, despite having no money and possibly no place to stay; he was quite relaxed and contented. Not a general description you'd use for your average homeless panhandler working the streets of Detroit. *How could he be like that?* I pondered as I walked, mechanically placing one foot in front of the other, my mind on this enigmatic man....

As I walked into my apartment block, hoping I wouldn't bump into my landlord, to whom I owed money, I heard the usual sounds of domestic arguments wafting through walls and down the corridors. It's always over something minor like "Woman! I said no goddamn sugar in my tea!" or "Where did you put my TV magazine, you sneaky bastard?!" But for some reason, to them, these trivial issues were worthy of screaming over, and throwing crockery or anything else in reachable distance, at each other. Hearing these arguments, the yelling, misplaced anger and angst, just thin walls away, confirmed to me that my life was at rock bottom.

I unlocked my apartment door and walked inside. The first thing I did was look at the answering machine. Maybe someone called...? As usual, the light wasn't flashing, a stark reminder of my loneliness and isolation from the world. I threw my keys on the table and switch on the TV. Tuesday night football blared out of the box, filling the apartment with loud and aggressive commentary, camouflaging the sounds of next door's violence. I walked to the kitchen to make some toasted cheese sandwiches. All the while, I couldn't stop thinking about the Beggar. Something about the old man in the filthy, tattered black coat struck a chord with me. For some reason, even though I scorned his appearance, something inside me made me look beyond the man's physical appearance. It was as if he had put a spell on me and injected a different perspective into my brain.

I placed the sandwiches on a plate and lay down with them on the bed in front of the TV, staring at the screen but not really paying attention to the TV or the hot food next to me. The sound from the TV floated over my head and became background noise as I began to sink into deep thoughts stemming from my bizarre encounter with the beggar, until eventually I drifted off to sleep.

The alarm clock sounded. It was 4:30 in the morning. As per usual, I was groaning in disappointment that it was time to get up. I was still tired and yearned to sleep a little more. My arm landed heavily on the clock's stop button with a sinking feeling in my stomach. That instant depression kicked in, the feeling of being fed up with everything, not looking forward to my day, plus the fear of instability and uncertainty. I hated that feeling. As I dragged myself to the bathroom, I mumbled to myself the words the beggar spoke to me. "I'm exactly where I'm supposed to be..."

Really?!

"Was I meant to be picking up rubbish and living below the poverty line? This is ridiculous!" I muttered to myself with discontentment before leaving my apartment to meet Joshua at the depot.

Upon arriving at the depot, Joshua was already there, wearing his usual large-sized smile and "positive outlook on life" badge, something that made me uncomfortable at times. Here's a family man, with far more responsibilities than I have, who is quite happy to work in stench day in, day out. Every day, he maintains a smile on his face, and rarely complains, unlike myself. This contrast between us made me feel a little uneasy.

"Good morning, Sam!" Joshua greeted me cheerfully. "You look like you had a rough night!"

"Thanks, Josh," I replied sarcastically. "To be honest, yesterday something strangely intense happened to me, and it turned out to be quite draining. I don't feel rested at all—"

Joshua interrupted abruptly. "Right! Someone had a happy meal?!"

I laughed at the excited look on his face. "I wish I did! But that's not the reason I'm so drained. Besides, you know me, Josh; how can I bring a woman to my neighborhood and into my crappy little shoebox apartment, complete with the real-life *Days of Our Lives* playing out next door?"

Joshua shook his head. "Man, seriously! You gotta stop thinking like that! You're not measured as a man by where you live and what you do. If she likes you, she'll like you as a garbage man..... or a beggar!"

"Yeah, right," I replied with my usual sarcasm, but his use of the beggar example didn't escape my notice. "I've already heard all the various forms of this cliché, but thanks anyway. From where I'm standing, having money is the key to having a happy life. It's the reason my childhood was nonexistent. If I win the lotto tomorrow, I'll show you how I solve every issue and obstacle in my life!" I punctuated my conviction with a wink.

"And speaking of beggars," I continued. "I had the most intriguing encounter with a beggar down at Elizabeth Park yesterday. He said some creepy stuff to me, which, by the way, is the reason I didn't get much sleep last night."

"That does sound intriguing!" Joshua looked at me carefully. "A beggar kept you awake last night? That's creepy alright!" he snickered. "How does a beggar keep you awake at night? Was he

29

singing you a serenade under your window?" He laughed that hearty chuckle of his.

"It's not so much the beggar himself, but what he said that kept me awake," I tried to explain over the noise of the engine, while throwing bags of rubbish into the back of the truck and tapping the side of the truck signalling the driver to move forward.

"Let me guess!" shouted Joshua, still chuckling. "He said, 'Do you have a quarter?'"

"Actually, he asked for a couple of dollars. Inflation, you see!" I laughed hard, and it felt good to laugh from the belly. "He didn't even look like he was desperate at all. In fact, he had this calming, grounded presence about him. But that's not what kept me awake. What kept me awake was that he knew my name and said he knew me."

Joshua suddenly stopped lifting the bin, and looked at me with a stunned expression on his face.

"Ohhhh boy!"

"What oh boy!?" I asked anxiously, struggling to understand his response. I knew it was a bizarre story but I didn't expect this level of reaction from Joshua.

"Never mind... What else did he say?" Joshua asked with increased interest. He slammed the bin back on the street and emptied the next one, all the while listening carefully.

"He just said that he knew where I was in my life. He said I was exactly where I needed to be. Strange isn't it?"

Joshua's face suddenly turned pale, and he had frozen in mid bin lift.

"Are you alright, Josh!?" I asked, more than a little concerned. I'd never seen Joshua behave like this.

"Yes, Sam, I'm okay. I just had a flashback moment. What else did he say?!" Joshua asked with a trembling voice, as if he were worried. He continued to work as I explained.

"Nothing much really. He just said that he knew where I was going, and something about knowing people through their energy field. He called it...wait a second, I forgot.... mmmm—"

"Aura," Joshua interrupted.

"That's it!" I exclaimed. "aura! He said that everyone has this magnetic field around them. He was going on about all kinds of new age mumbo jumbo, energy, abundance, and nonmaterialism... Hogwash if you ask me," I finished cynically, and tipped two bins into the truck with top precision.

"Actually, Sam, he's right!" Joshua jumped in before I could continue. "The aura can be sometimes described as the map of thoughts and feelings a person entertains. Good to see someone's giving you some profound life lessons, Sam," Joshua said soberly.

"Profound?!" I protested. "Is this part of that Universe bliss thing that you do? Don't forget that this 'profound' lesson came from a beggar," I reminded him.

31

"So?!" Joshua exclaimed. "What's wrong with advice from a beggar?"

"So?!" I exclaimed with equal passion. "It's a bit ironic that profound life lessons would come from a man who begs for money and lives on the streets, don't you think?"

Joshua's face suddenly turned serious as if he were about to give a sermon.

"Do you consider yourself an intelligent man, Sam?"

"I'm pretty sure I am!" I replied with a cocky smile, lifting another two bins and emptying them out.

Joshua put down the trash can he was about to tip into the truck.

"Some people might look at you, and think that you're not very intelligent because you're a garbage collector. Do you believe that you lost your intelligence when you became a garbage collector? Did you lose your intelligence when you had no home to go to? This man didn't forget his life lessons all of a sudden when he became a beggar. In fact, he may just have some valuable lessons to share," Joshua added, winking kindly.

I had to admit that I was pretty much cornered by Joshua's comment. He was right, and I, for a change, had no comeback for this one. I just nodded and continued tipping the garbage cans into the truck.

For the rest of our shift, Joshua wasn't his usual happy self. He kept looking at me strangely as if he knew something I didn't. He continued working, tipping the garbage cans into the truck at his usual pace, but not saying much.

At the end of the shift, Joshua patted me on the back, looked me in the eye and said, "Good job today, son; I'll see you tomorrow."

"Is everything okay?" I asked.

"Everything is perfect," he said with a wide smile on his face, walking toward his car.

I stood there for a minute longer, watching Joshua walk away. I wondered what happened to him. He seemed very strange, almost disturbed, after I told him about the beggar. I thought maybe I had said something to offend him, but, knowing Joshua, it's not possible that he would shut down and not tell me if I had said something out of line or offensive. Joshua is a man who isn't fazed by much, and that made me even more curious about his strong reaction to my story.

I decided to walk home via the produce market, and pick up some groceries. It's a weekly market for overstocked vendors to move leftover produce they haven't sold. It's a very popular market, particularly amongst the low-income families, because they get a lot of produce for half the price. The market was crowded. I had never seen it so crowded before, and the atmosphere there was really special. I love hearing all the various vendors plugging their products, each in their own style and theatrical voice. Some even create a flow of poetry around their product to try and entice customers to stop, listen, and then buy from them. I like to call it a shopping experience with entertainment.

I usually know what I'm shopping for, and I'll head straight to the stalls I like, but sometimes, I enjoy having a look around if I have the time and patience, and soak up the atmosphere. When it's crowded, I often bump shoulders with passers by. It requires a certain level of skill and agility to manoeuver around people and avoid bumping into them. I picked up some tomatoes and a bag of potatoes from one of the vendors I frequent every week and as I turned to walk away from the stall, I bumped straight into a woman, carrying a box of apples. The apples rolled all over the ground.

She was flustered and groused, "You clumsy monkey! Watch where you're going!"

"Oops, sorry!" I said to the woman sheepishly, while frantically trying to pick up as many apples as I could without being stomped on by the dozen pairs of legs around me. "I'm really sorry," I apologized again to her, and turned away toward the exit.

As I looked ahead, trying to wiggle my way through the crowd, about a quarter of a block away dead ahead, there he was, the beggar. He was standing there looking directly into my eyes as if I were the only person there. I could feel his deep blue eyes penetrating mine from that distance. He stared directly at me, and gave me a creepy smile.

"What the hell?!" I exclaimed to myself out loud.

"This is the beggar I met in the park yesterday. He's looking directly at me," I continued my internal dialogue. "Is he stalking me?" I started striding toward him, bumping into people with a little less care. I wanted to get to him as quickly as possible. The bag of potatoes I was carrying burst open and all the potatoes fell on the ground, but I didn't care, I just kept striding toward him. My view was intermittently blocked by the crowd, but I kept my eyes directly on where he was standing, increasing my pace whenever I could, but just as I got to the corner where he was standing, he disappeared.

I looked to the left and to the right in confusion, but on both sides, there was a fence. There was no way a man of his age could have snuck away so quickly over the fence. "Where did he go?" I found myself asking myself repeatedly. I was stunned. I started to wonder if I were hallucinating. I stood there trembling inside my skin, the noise from the market started to fade away from consciousness, and in my head I could almost hear my heart beat. *This can't be,* I thought to myself. How could he disappear like that? The place is fenced off, and, unless he could fly, there was no way he could escape from sight like that. But he did. He just vanished.

I walked out of the market grounds, still looking around, trying to spot the beggar. Maybe he dodged me somehow, but I couldn't see him anywhere.
This is the kind of elusive magic you see in the movies, I thought to myself. I started walking home, all the while on the lookout, trying to spot the beggar...
I just couldn't wrap my head around what had transpired. I knew I saw him. People don't just vanish like that. This wasn't a Walt Disney movie I'd been cast in, and I would hate to consider that I was hallucinating the whole thing... Yet, what was the alternative....? A magician beggar? One who could move with more agility and lightning speed than a ninja?!

My heart was pounding at an uncomfortable rate; I was walking like a drunken person, not paying attention to where I staggered. I just kept turning my head randomly in an attempt to spot the beggar, to prove that I wasn't hallucinating, that disappearing people is only something

35

you see in movies and that he had been hiding in a doorway this whole time. But no matter how long I staggered around in hopeful desperation, he was still nowhere to be seen.

I finally gave up and headed for home, realizing that I hadn't actually bought anything. I'd lost a bag of potatoes when I was chasing the beggar, and since witnessing his great disappearance, my mind was totally thrown. I had completely forgotten to buy the groceries I needed to make dinner. Wearily, I entered my apartment, grabbed a bag of potato chips on the kitchen table, and sat in front of the TV, turning it up loud enough to drown out the arguing that was seeping through my walls. I'm so sick of this style of living. I need a serious change. Maybe I was losing my mind and wasn't aware of it. Maybe thinking that I saw the beggar vanish was a sign that my sanity was slipping away from me. My mind split into two schools of thought: the rational and irrational. The rational said that I knew that I saw him. He looked directly into my eyes and smiled, as if he were saying, "I see you." But the irrational thought process said that maybe he did indeed vanish.

I started to panic, but that led to the familiar sensation of utter confusion that followed yesterday's exchange. I was so physically tired, I lay in bed, trying to fall asleep, but between my hunger and my brain in total overdrive, sleeping proved very challenging.

"Bloody hell!" I said to myself out loud. "Not another sleepless night because of that damned beggar." I was angry. Angry at the beggar and at myself for being unable to make sense of things. The pill bottles were still on the bedside table. As I looked at them, I was tempted to gobble them down and just put an end to it once and for all. But my curiosity about the beggar got the better of me, and I decided to postpone it for a day.

36

My imagination was rampant. I started running scenarios through my head in an effort to make sense of it all. First, he claimed to have known me. Then he knew my name, and now he is watching me through a huge crowd and vanishes. This isn't something I can comprehend. I can't even begin to make sense of it....

Tomorrow is my day off. I decided to go down to the park along the river and look for the beggar. I had to see him before I lost my mind, and, this time, I wanted answers.

Chapter 3

Looking for the Beggar

The next morning, I got up around eight o'clock, after I managed to squeeze in a few hours of sleep, but my mind was still mulling over the disappearing beggar. I made some coffee and sat at the kitchen table just wondering into the air. I wanted to get down to the park as soon as possible; then the doorbell rang.

"Mr. King, are you there?" It was my landlord, probably trying to collect his rent. Then another knock. "Mr King!" he yelled.

I wasn't going to open the door. I've been trying to avoid him for days because I don't have his rent money until the next payday, and now I have to wait for him to leave, so I can get out of the apartment. He gave up on me, but I could still hear him knocking on other doors. "Damn! This man is like clockwork with his rent collection routine," I muttered.

I tiptoed to the door, so he wouldn't hear the creak of the floorboards, and put my ear to the door, waiting for him to move along so I can get out of the apartment without having to go through the humiliation of giving him another excuse for having no money for rent. When I couldn't hear him no more, I opened the door slightly and peered through to the corridor to see if he'd gone, but I could still hear murmurs coming from the floor below, so I decided to stay in for a while longer and wait for a safe escape window.

When the opportunity finally came, I crept out of the apartment, making my way through the corridors and stairwells like a navy seal on a mission to take over a terrorist's building, peering carefully around each corner, making sure he wasn't still lurking around.

I finally made it out of the building, crossed the road to further stay out of sight, and ran toward the park. It was another beautiful day, but I wasn't paying attention to anything around me. It wasn't my usual walk of contemplation and admiration of the view, or fantasizing about Selena. I was a man on a mission to find the beggar. I couldn't stand another sleepless night, or to further drain my brain over this. I had to find him, and that was the only thing on my agenda.

The park was busier than usual, which could be good because maybe the beggar prefers busier days, better for begging I thought. I walked straight to the spot where I'd first met him a couple of days ago. Next to the yellow park bench. When I got there, a couple was sitting on the bench, but the beggar wasn't there. I walked up to them to ask them if they have seen the beggar.

"Hi, good morning, sorry to bother you. Did you happen to see a beggar, wearing a black coat, long hair, gray beard?"

The man laughed and said, "You just described all the beggars I know. Do you think you could narrow it down a little?"

"Doesn't matter," I said and smiled. "Thanks!"

"Good luck!" the man wished upon me. I smiled and walked toward Joe, the hotdog vendor. He was setting up his stand, getting ready to sell.

"Morning, Joe! Getting ready for a lot of business?"

"Morning, Sam! Yeah, I agree with the 'getting ready' part, don't know about the 'lot of business part," he replied, chuckling. "These days everyone wants low sugar, low fat, low salt, low everything. They're starting to see me as the enemy of the health club and try to avoid me." He laughed and grabbed a bun, pointed it at me and said, "Breakfast for champions?!"

Joe calls eating a hotdog early in the morning breakfast for champions. It's the practice of introducing a hotdog to an empty stomach first thing in the morning.

"No thanks," I declined politely. "I'm actually on a mission to find a certain beggar."

"Well, there are plenty here," Joe said, laughing.

"Did you see me talking to a beggar the other day?" I asked.

"No, sorry, Sam."

"He was wearing a black coat, and had a gray beard," I said.

"To me, they all look the same, Sam, but I saw a beggar walking past a while ago; he went there." Joe pointed down the promenade.

"Okay, thanks, Joe. I'll see you later. Hope the health club don't come knocking," I joked.

I started walking toward where Joe pointed, hoping it was "my" beggar whom he saw earlier. I walked all the way to the end of the promenade, but the beggar was nowhere to be seen. In my mind, I kept asking, *Where are you? Where are you?* As I looked in all directions. After all, a beggar shouldn't be too hard to spot. I looked everywhere, but to no avail. I must have picked the wrong day to be looking for him, maybe he begged in a different spot each time, and today wasn't "park day."
Disappointed, I leaned over the guardrail, looking at the water. I was just focusing on the small ripples down below and admiring the reflection of the sun's rays over the water, when suddenly I felt an immense power making me want to turn around. It felt like I couldn't resist it. I turned around, but there was nothing behind me. As I looked up ahead, there he was, sitting under a tree in a lotus position, again looking right at me, the same way he looked at me in the market.

He gave me that same creepy smile and I felt chills down my spine again. I was a little apprehensive this time around. This whole idea of this man seemingly just following me around, and looking directly at me, as if I were the most interesting thing in the whole world, was making me a little nervous and defensive, but, nonetheless, I had to find out what the hell was going on with this beggar. Why was he

41

watching me? How did he know my name? And why did he say he knew me?

I started to walk toward him, thinking, *I hope he doesn't disappear on me again*, even though it would have been quite obvious if he did, since there weren't as many people in the park as there were at the market to block my view to him. This was my only rational explanation to his disappearance at the market, that maybe he walked around the crowd, and somehow dodged me. Whatever it was, I felt a little irritated by this and wanted answers

As I approached the tree he was sitting against, I couldn't help noticing his deep blue eyes again, There was something soothing about them, I couldn't quite explain why, but all I know is, by the time I got closer to him, my irritation had dissipated, and a sense of calmness took over me.

"Hi, Sam," he greeted, "I've been expecting you."

"You've been expecting me?" I asked surprised. "Do you mean you've been expecting me because you knew I'd want to know why you're following me?"

The beggar chuckled, straightening that half-smoked cigarette again.

"Do you ever smoke that thing?" I asked.

"Do you have a light?" he asked with a cheeky grin on his face.

"No! I don't smoke, I told you," I replied impatiently.

"Then it doesn't look like I'll be smoking it," he replied laughing.

"Look! All I want to know is, why are you following me?" I asked with an increased assertiveness.

"What makes you think that I'm following you, Sam? Aren't you the one looking for me?!" He chuckled.

"Y...Yeah," I said, stammering slightly. "But you were at the outdoor market yesterday, looking straight at me, and then you just disappeared! How did you disappear?! The place was fenced off. Can you fly?! How did you know my name?" I kept insisting.

"Okay, Sam, I understand you have a lot of questions; so, for now, I'll just say that your father asked me to look after you."

"You knew my father?" I asked surprised.

"I did and still do," said the beggar.

"You do know he's dead, right?" I said.

"Yes, I do," he replied. "My condolences; I know you adored him a lot," he said compassionately.

"I don't understand! My father asked a beggar to look after me? This doesn't make sense!" I started to feel that maybe this whole thing with the beggar was some kind of candid camera show, or maybe someone was pulling a sick joke on me.

"I don't mean to offend you, mister," I said. "But how is a beggar going to look after me? Were you a beggar when my father asked you to look after me before he died? Because I doubt it very much that he would ask a beggar to look after me; again, no offense."

"None taken, Sam," he said, smiling.

"Your father asked me to look after you when the time was right, and now is the time," the beggar said.

"How so?" I asked with a defiant tone.

"Because you're on the verge of a breaking point from which there may be no return," the beggar said softly, while looking straight into my eyes, piercing me with his deep blue eyes again. I'm not usually drawn to eyes, but this man was different. His eyes were as blue as the ocean, and not just the iris, but the sclera, which is usually white, had a tint of blue in it as well. It was almost hypnotic. I tried hard to ignore it and maintain my tough disposition by saying with a slight scorn in my voice, "And you would know this how?"

"You'll know how soon enough," said the beggar.

"Oh, that's right! That aura thing, right?!" I scoffed. "You did say that one can tell a lot about someone without even knowing them, if I remember correctly. So now you see through my aura and by the way I carry myself, that I'm on the verge of a breaking point." I kept my sarcastic voice. "And I suppose that's how you knew my name; my aura told you, right!?"

"That's right," he said with a cheeky grin on his face.

"This is insane!" I protested. "I came here to find you, to get some answers, and now I'm more confused than before I had the questions."

The beggar laughed and said, "That's okay, Sam; I have a lot of time for you. What questions do you have for me?"

"Well, again," I said impatiently, "how did you do a disappearing act on me at the market yesterday? I know I saw you, but you just disappeared! That's impossible."

The beggar laughed and said, "The mind can sometimes see things it wants to see, and make things vanish when it doesn't want to see them."

"That's very philosophical, sir, but it doesn't make sense," I insisted.

"Sure it does. I promise you, Sam; you'll understand soon enough. Have patience," the beggar said.

"Patience is a virtue I don't possess," I said, while becoming slightly irate.

"I know!" The beggar chuckled.

"Very funny!" I said obnoxiously.

"Patience is a virtue most people don't possess, yet it's one of the main ingredients to a happy peaceful life, so don't be too hard on yourself," he said.

"Yeah, patience maybe okay for a beggar," I replied with my usual cocky voice. "Obviously, you have all the time in the world with nothing to do and nowhere to go."

The beggar smiled and chuckled. "I do have all the time in the world, Sam. Any more questions?"

"Do you have a name? Since you know mine, I thought maybe I should know yours."

"Sure I do. I'm Gabe; nice to meet you, again."

"Gabe?! I don't recall my father having a friend called Gabe, and if he asked you to look after me, that means you were close and I would have known you. How come you never visited when he was sick?"

"Oh, I visited your father many times; it's just that you were never there to witness it." Gabe lowered his head and said in a soft voice, "Your father was a good man, Sam. He was very proud of you. You were his pillar of strength, and you should always remember that."

"Thanks!" I replied. "It's just that I don't understand why he would ask a beggar to look after me. Does it look like I need looking after? With all due respect, what kind of role model are you? It doesn't look like you can look after yourself, let alone someone else. Again, no offense."

"Again, none taken," Gabe replied, chuckling. "He did warn me about you being a stubborn young man, and cocky at times."

"Well, you can't blame me for questioning these dynamics," I replied.

"It's okay, son," Gabe said softly. "You were born into a world that gives accolades to those who accumulate wealth, and looks down upon those who don't have much, and I understand that. So now, you're looking at me, judging me by my appearance, and you don't believe that I could possibly be of any use to you. This is the blinding effect of the material world."

"Blinding effect of the material world. That sounds very profound, sir, but the reality is, in this world, if you don't have money, you're subjected to a life of struggle and minimal opportunities. It's why my father couldn't get the best treatment, and why I had to give up a normal childhood. I had to leave school so I could work to help keep food on the table and pay his medical bills. I've seen and lived the effects of not having money firsthand. Now, all I'm qualified to do is garbage collection because I have no degree and I can't afford to get a degree. So don't just sit there and tell me it's blinding. Just look at you; if you had money, you'd be sleeping in a bed and not on the street. You wouldn't have to beg people for money. So, if this is blinding, then I'd rather not see."

"What makes you believe that you're only qualified to work as a garbage collector?" Gabe asked.

"In this material world, as you like to call it, people are hired based on their qualifications and experience. I've applied for numerous jobs in various fields, and I was turned down for all of them simply because I never finished school and don't have a degree or experience," I said.

"And you had experience in garbage collection?" Gabe asked.

"No, you don't need experience in lifting garbage cans, but it was better than nothing, since I used to be like you," I replied.

"Like me?" Gabe asked in a surprised voice.

"Yes, like you. I was homeless once, and I resorted to collecting and selling aluminium cans as a means to make some money. It was only by chance that I got the job as a garbage collector. I was lucky I suppose. Right place at the right time if you will."

"Do you really believe that it was by chance that you got the job, Sam?"

I laughed sarcastically and said, "I'm 100% sure it was by chance. In fact, if it weren't for my muscles, I probably wouldn't have been offered the job either. The depot manager even said that he can use someone like me because of my strong build; otherwise, I probably would still be collecting cans and sleeping in a shelter."

"What if I told you it wasn't by chance, Sam?"

"Well, if it wasn't by chance, then it was sheer luck," I replied.

"I agree that you were there at the right time or, more accurately, the right timing. But It wasn't by chance, and it wasn't by sheer luck. It was your destiny. It was where you needed to be," said Gabe.

I scoffed. "Are you serious?! My destiny is to be a garbage collector?"

"Your destiny isn't one defined event or job; your destiny is what you're here to accomplish and experience from the cradle to the grave. This was just a piece of the puzzle. You were meant to get this garbage job in order to move on to the next experience, whatever it may be. It's a steppingstone if you will, and the road is long, so buckle up!" he said, laughing.

"I'm not sure I'm with you on that one, mister. I've had nothing but grief and bad luck so far. My mother left us, my father died suffering, I was homeless, and now I live below the poverty line while doing something I hate. Is this destiny? If this is my destiny, then I don't want to live," I said.

"From the ego's perspective, it may seem like that. But from your soul's perspective, this is exactly what needed to happen," said Gabe.

"Well then, the soul is very cruel if that's what it has done to me—"

"Actually," Gabe interrupted, "it's the ego that's cruel. The ego is what gives you false hopes and dreams. It makes you believe that you're here to work hard and accumulate material wealth in order to have a happy fulfilled life, but, in the process, you miss out on the real experiences you came here to experience."

"Well, I much rather be unhappy with material wealth than unhappy without," I said.

Gabe laughed. "If you only knew how many people discovered that winning the lottery was the worst thing that ever happened to them, you'd be rethinking that statement."

"I doubt that very much," I replied with a cocky tone.

"Don't underestimate the power of the brainwashing," said Gabe. "This brainwashing started from the time you were born; it's responsible for most of your distorted outlook on life."

"What brainwashing?" I asked.

"The brainwashing that conditioned you to believe that you are nothing, unless you have something," said Gabe. He then pointed at a black Porche driving pass. "Do you think the person inside that Porche is happier than you?"

"He definitely doesn't have to worry about not having enough to pay bills," I scoffed. "And he definitely doesn't have a landlord who demands his rent not a minute after its due. So yes, I think he's happier," I said.

Gabe laughed. "And you assume all this just by looking at the car he drives? If you remembered what you knew when you were born, none of this would even phase you. When you were born, you knew exactly who you were and what you were here to do. It was only when you started living from an ego perspective and entered the realm of the ego world that you forgot who you really were and what was most important. Your whole makeup was changed, and you were given a character, which is the mask you use to define yourself and fit yourself into this holographic reality you were given. This is why you think that the man in the Porche is happier and doesn't have any worries because, in the ego world, it's a status symbol of happiness and a source of envy."

"The ego world?" I asked surprised.

"The false self," Gabe replied.

"Sorry, Gabe, I don't think I follow."

"When you were born, you were complete. You had a path planned for you, and the knowing of how to get there. You then were raised within a society that taught you about trends, put emphasis on the importance of being cool. You've been bombarded with media imagery, celebrity influence, and peer group pressure, and, of course, organized religions that taught you that you have no power unless you turn to their indoctrination and externalised your spiritual makeup, using fear of punishment and death. That made you believe that you're just a random number among many who needs to fight for a place on this earth with no purpose and no destiny. This is your false self. But your main purpose is actually something else, something far more profound. You simply forgot who you really are, but your soul remembers, and it'll pull you back onto your path whenever you veer off it," said Gabe.

"Well, we can just undo it, can't we?" I asked.

"Sounds easy enough," said Gabe. "But first you need to know that you can undo it. This brainwashing reshaped your belief system, your knowing, as well as your spiritual power, to a point where you simply let yourself drown because you don't know that you're a natural swimmer."

"So is your main purpose being a beggar?" I asked with a cocky tone.

"Sam, it may surprise you, but I used to be a very wealthy man," said Gabe with a chuckle.

"I find that very hard to believe," I replied.

"Yes, I was. I used to be Gabriel Taylor, the CEO of T.R. Chem. The T stands for Taylor. I had cars, a mansion with a swimming pool, housekeepers, and even a yearly membership at an exclusive golf club. I had it all." Gabe laughed.

"T.R. Chem?!" I exclaimed. "THE' T.R. Chem?! The biggest chemical company in the world?! I don't understand! What happened to you?" I asked surprised.

"I decided to abandon my life," Gabe winked at me.

"You abandoned your life in favor of beggary?" I asked, surprised.

"Pretty much! But being a beggar was my choice and not a consequence of bad luck or hardship." Gabe laughed.

"Ahh....Nah! Sorry, Gabe, I don't believe you!" I objected.

"Of course you don't believe me." Gabe laughed. "To you, it's crazy. How can anyone give up the very thing you believe is the solution to your unhappiness and be happy being where you fear to be the most, Right?"

"Very eloquent, Gabe, and you're right." I laughed. "Most people work very hard to have what you've supposedly given up."

"Most people think that their mission in life is to accumulate wealth," said Gabe. "I've been there, and I was very unhappy still. When you don't live your intended path, it's like a thirst you cannot quench. I had phoney friends and money to buy their opinions and admiration. But that was ego satisfying, and it left me empty inside. My soul was pulling me in another direction, which was the reason I felt unhappy, because I wasn't in alignment with my destiny. It's only when I thought I had it all that it became obvious that I actually had nothing.

I never knew who was genuinely there for me and who was there because of my money and influence. I lived a life of constant suspicion and paranoia. Does the woman I'm with truly love me? Or is she really there for my money and is really in love with my status? Those were the questions I asked myself all the time, until I couldn't recognize my life anymore. I couldn't distinguish between the false me and the true me, and that's the worse place you can be."

"Wow! This is a little hard to get my head around, Gabe. No offense. I just can't see the purpose in being a beggar."

"A beggar gives people an opportunity to express generosity, which is one of the acts of love many people wish to express," Gabe explained, chuckling.

"Very cute!" I said sarcastically. "But with all due respect, I don't see you drowning in coins here."

"That's because I don't need them right now," Gabe said.

"You don't need coins?!" I asked surprised. "Isn't that the reason you're begging?"

"When you're on your intended path, everything you need is provided for you when it's needed," explained Gabe.

"It seems to me that this intended path has eluded me somehow," I said sarcastically.

"What makes you think that?" Gabe asked.

"Because I have no idea where to go and what to do with my life. I feel so lost and hopeless," I said shakily.

"And what makes you think that you're not living it now, and that where you are is exactly where you need to be right now?" Gabe asked.

"Because I don't feel secure right now. I'm sick of worrying about losing my job whenever I go into work. I'm sick of losing sleep, worrying that I might end up living on the streets again. I thought garbage collecting would be temporary, until I found something better, but three years later, I'm still doing the same thing. I feel I have so much more potential and so much more to offer," I said with a choked voice.

"And this is why patience is an important virtue," said Gabe softly. "Sam, we all live in a linear timeframe. An hour is sixty minutes, a day is twenty-four hours, a year is 365 days, and we tend to measure our life achievements and accomplishments based on these time units. People say, 'I'm almost thirty, I have to get married before I'm too old' or 'I should be financially sound by the time I'm thirty-five.' They work themselves up, trying to rush through life, based on a linear system of time. The Universe, however, doesn't operate according to these time units. The universe operates with milestones, but there's no timeframe to each milestone. When you're ready to jump to your next milestone, it will happen, regardless of how many days or years have passed. The ego, once again, is trying to trick you into thinking that you're stuck. It's trying to trick you into thinking that you must do something, but it has no idea what to do. Your soul, however, knows that the end of the milestone will be reached naturally, and it's ready to connect with the next one. Be patient. You don't need to push the river; the river is moving on its own." Gabe smiled.

"I just want it to happen already!" I said with a childish tantrum. "I deserve a better life!"

Gabe smiled and said, "A better life depends on your perception between the milestones. When you're driving from Detroit to Chicago, you can worry and stress that the road is too long, that you might run out of gas, and that maybe you're lost, or you can trust that you'll eventually reach Chicago, regardless of the emotions you chose to entertain, and enjoy the scenery instead. That's the beauty of being led through life, because when you're led into something, you're also guaranteed to be led out of it and into the next with very little effort on your part."

"So how do I find my intended path?" I asked with a cheeky voice. "Do I just open a map?"

Gabe laughed, clasped his hands together behind his head, and leaned back on the tree, saying, "Your map is already loaded into you, Sam; you just need to trust the signs that are pointing the way and follow them."

"Signs? Like a Treasure Trove game?" I said.

"Exactly!" Gabe exclaimed cheerfully. "Only a lot more advanced. The Universe constantly gives you directions and signs about where to go and what to do, but you either don't notice them or don't trust them. Remember the brainwashing?"

"I still don't quite get what you mean by brainwashing. Are you saying that someone is messing with our heads?" I asked.

"The matrix you're living in isn't real. It's a holographic construct that's based on fear, materialism, and egotism. Above this illusionary layer, there's another layer of your higher self. It's your soul, Sam, and your soul is the driver of your life, because it knows who you really are, and where you need to go. Your body is the vehicle and your ego is the backseat driver that's always complaining." Gabe chuckled before he continued.

"You were conditioned to believe that who you are equals what you possess. You were conditioned to believe that in order to have knowledge, you need experts to tell you what's right and wrong, what's good and bad. Most of us grew up under some form of religious indoctrination that we have no power within us, and that an all-powerful external God will punish us if we don't obey his rules. This made you forget who you are and that you actually possess the tools you need to follow your destined path." Gabe nodded

"Are you saying there's no God?" I asked surprised.

"Not in the sense most people think of," Gabe said. "We all were made to think that God is an outside entity who lives in the heavens and watches everything we do. This belief created polarization between believers and unbelievers and nurtured fear within us. This couldn't be further from the truth; trust me!" Gabe chuckled.

"Hmm... I'm confused. Who is God, then?" I asked.

"God isn't a 'who' or a 'what.' God is a collective of souls. It's you and everybody else. It's what connects us all. To believe that we all

56

are separate and alone is like thinking that the ocean is composed of zillions of separate drops of water. A drop that's separated from the ocean is weak and powerless but all drops united with the ocean can wear down mountains. We are all one, Sam, no separation whatsoever, and we're stronger when we're connected together," Gabe said, nodding

"We're all one?" I exclaimed. "Have you seen the state of the world lately? We're hating each other, killing each other, ridiculing each other. That's hardly a unity, don't you think?"

"Yes, Sam, I've seen it. That's the result of not understanding this simple truth. "How hard would it be for me to convince you that a drop out of a glass full of the same water is actually made of different components?" Gabe asked.

"Very hard! You won't convince me," I said with conviction.

"That's right!" Gabe replied. "So think how much went into convincing you that you're separate from everybody else and that you're made of different components."

"Was it the teachers and doctors who made us believe this?" I asked.

"Teachers and doctors are conveyors of information; they don't research the information they convey to their students or patients. They, just like you, agreed to it because they trusted the information was true. This can lead people down the path of ignorance. It simply blinds them to the truth about who they really are and what they're capable of." Gabe looked up and pointed at a bird, saying, "Do you think that bird had a teacher that taught it how to fly and how to find food and survive the cold?"

"No, of course not," I said, laughing.

"Then how is it surviving? Where did it get the knowledge on how to survive?"

"Hmm... good point," I said.

Gabe continued, "The point is, Sam, that this bird was born with all it needed to know in order to survive as a bird. But because it didn't have anything that interfered with its knowing, it remained intact. We were also born with the inner knowing on how to survive as humans and what our purpose is in this life. However, this knowing has been taken away from us by pointing us to experts who supposedly know what's best for us, how we should do things, and how we're supposed to think. This made us doubt our inner knowing, until we forgot it all together."

"This is all too confusing!" I protested. "How can I know what my path is then? How can I know my purpose if it's all suppressed?"

"It's in your passions," said Gabe. "It's what you're drawn to the most, your desires, and what inspires you. Those feelings are road signs to where you need to go and what you need to do. The holographic matrix can't take those away; it can only make you unaware of them, make you fantasize about them, or make you want to go against them."

I immediately thought about my dream of owning a restaurant, my fantasies about Selena, and winning the lottery.

"If you didn't feel inspired to do something, you wouldn't do it. In order to make you do something, your soul, which is your higher self, sends an inspiration as a signal to do it, and, sometimes, it puts you through certain situations that make you act in a certain way. It's like a game of Treasure Trove as you said. You get an assignment, and you need to act on it to get to the next milestone. So, life's a big game of puzzle, which you unravel a bit at the time, and it all happens in Universe time, not human linear time." Gabe smiled and nodded. "Patience. Sam, patience." he winked.

"Well, I'm very drawn to money," I said. "Why don't I have it or feel inspired to find it?"

Gabe started laughing.

"What's so funny?" I asked.

"Who's desiring it? Your soul? Or your ego?"

"What's the difference? Didn't you say that our desires are a sign that we're on our path?" I asked, sounding as cocky as usual.

"The desire you have for money is fear-based. It's your ego telling you that money is the reason you have these hardships. Your soul will never desire money as its main objective. The desires that come from your soul are based on love and service. They're a part of your true path and are based on what's best for you at that time to continue toward your next milestone. You see, Sam, your soul knows where you're going, and it knows that you have nothing to fear about your journey. But your ego doesn't trust that you'll be okay and makes you believe that your life is just a series of random events, but it's not.

Each event in your life has a purpose and is connected to other events that will eventually complete the puzzle. Do you understand?"

"I'm not sure I do. It all seems a little mystical to me," I said. "Looking at my life, I can't see how any pieces of a puzzle lead to a treasure."

Gabe nodded in sympathy. "I understand that you can't see any correlation between all the events in your life so far, and that's exactly what the ego does. For the ego, the only means of success is by receiving what it wants in term of financial rewards, accolades, admiration, materialism, and the like. This is the only way the ego feels satisfied. Your path may seemingly involve hardships and hurdles, but when you follow your true path, these hurdles become guides. Let me ask you this, Sam. How did you get the job at the garbage depot?"

"I told you, I went there to cash in the cans I had collected, and the manager spotted me and offered me a job," I said.

"And why did the manager offer you the job," Gabe continued to challenge.

"He thought he could use someone with muscles like mine," I said as I flexed my biceps to demonstrate. "I got these from working out at the gym."

"And why did you join the gym?" Gabe asked.

"Well, I needed something to take my mind off the problems at home, and training at the gym gave me the stress relief I needed."

Gabe nodded again and said, "So the problems at home inspired you to go to the gym, which made you muscular, which, in turn, got the depot manager's attention, yes?"

"That's one way of looking at it," I said.

"And how did you come up with the idea to collect and sell aluminium cans?" Gabe asked.

"It just came to me," I said. "I used to see homeless people do it in movies, so it just jumped into my head."

"And this enabled you to find a place to live, and get off the streets right?" Gabe continued.

"Yeah! What's your point?!" I asked with slight irritation.

"Do you think they were all random events that had no purpose? Or do you see how all these seemingly random events got you to where you are now and helped you get off the streets? Your sudden urge to sell aluminium cans wasn't by chance; it was guidance from your higher self, sending you inspiration to do it, and because this was part of your path, you naturally had no resistance doing it."

"Okay," I said. "That's a very nice way of looking at it, but you can't tell me that the reason my mother left us and my father had a serious ailment was to help me find a room in a derelict apartment block, can you?"

Gabe laughed and said, "From an ego perspective, those were just random disastrous events. The soul, however, put them in place, as steppingstones to its purpose. It put these events in place to help you find your true path and acquire the lessons and inner strength needed for the next stage of your life."

"This is crazy," I retorted. "Why can't my soul just lead me to a pot of gold? Why go through heartbreaking experiences just so I can find a room in a derelict apartment block? This doesn't make sense!"

"Sure it does, Sam. It makes perfect sense. Your life's mission isn't about finding a pot of gold. It's a spiritual journey. Believe it or not, Sam, not everyone was meant to be wealthy. Can you imagine what the world would be like if everyone who wanted to be wealthy was wealthy? There would be no need for generosity. Who would want to work as a clerk or a sales attendant? It's like having a world with daylight only but not night or with only ups but not downs or having chefs only but no diners. For some, being wealthy isn't part of their journey and not part of their destiny, and by constantly chasing it, they waste their lives chasing something that isn't supposed to be theirs. The ones who achieved great wealth did so by pursuing their true passions, regardless of whether it would yield them large amounts of money or not. It was part of their destiny. Their purpose was primarily to create something that was of service to everyone; it was what they were meant to do in this lifetime, and they had the inspiration and the drive to accomplish their purpose. This drive comes naturally to those who are on their intended path. The money is only a by-product of that. Those who just want to make money find that, sooner or later, they run out of steam and fail or get bored and unhappy, just like I did."

Chapter 4

Follow Your Passions

I looked at Gabe with fearful eyes as he said those words. "Do you mean to say that I was destined to be poor for the rest of my life?"

"Not necessarily," said Gabe. "What I meant to say is, follow your passions and live your life, knowing that when you're on your intended path, you'll have everything you need in order to live in peace. Poverty is the way your ego interprets not having money. Abundance is the soul's way of saying that you'll have what you need, when you need it in order to complete your intended journey, and that requires a lot of trust. Your ego will do whatever it can to scare you off of that trust, so be mindful of that," said Gabe.

"That's great!" I said sarcastically. "So now I'm supposed to just accept my living conditions as a gift?"

"No, you should look at what's happening in your life, as meaningful events that lead you to your destiny, rather than meaningless events that are random strings of bad luck. "What do you feel inspired to do, Sam?" Gabe asked.

"I always dreamed of having my own restaurant," I said.

"Why do you want to have your own restaurant?"

"After seeing poverty first hand and how most poor people can't afford to eat out, I came up with an idea for a place that serves quality tasty food that's for everyone, regardless of whether or not they can afford it," I said.

"Wow!" Gabe exclaimed. "You didn't say it was because you wanted to make lots of money. That's noble. And that's what I'm talking about, Sam! You've just described a possible purpose to your life, the way your soul would describe it, and far from the ego. But why aren't you pursuing your restaurant dream then?"

I scoffed, "Get real, Gabe! You need money to set up a restaurant, and, right now, I can hardly scrap enough money for a sandwich."

Gabe smiled, shook his head, and said, "This is one of the main reasons most people never chase their dreams. They let themselves down through assumptions like that, but they never consider that the reason they had this dream in the first place was because their higher self is sending them a message through inspiration to go and do it."

"Well, smart guy! How do you suggest I open a restaurant with no money?" I asked sarcastically.

"Pay more attention," said Gabe.

"Pay attention to what?" I asked.

"Pay attention to what's happening around you. Your higher self is giving you directions on how to get there, but because your ego tricks you to think that unless you have money, you won't be able to achieve your dream, you dismiss synchronistic events and situations that are supposed to lead you to accomplishing your dream through other means. That's why it's called 'higher self' because it stands above the minutia and routine of daily life and can see a wider view of your path from above," said Gabe.

"Forgive my scepticism! How exactly is my higher self giving me directions?" I asked.

"Again, pay attention to the signs," said Gabe. "Remember the map that's already installed within you? That map has your journey all mapped out for you, and your higher self is at the helm of your ship. It sends you directions through inspiration and the so-called synchronicities. It arranges situations and events in your life, and you need to act upon them. It's called 'cooperation'; you and the universe are cooperating in a joint venture to guide you through your journey. Most people dismiss them as meaningless coincidences, but nothing in your life is a meaningless coincidence. Every person you meet, every situation you encounter, and even the people you don't like or perceive as bad have a purpose for your life. When you understand this, you won't hate anything or anyone. You'll understand that all things are connected and all events lead somewhere for your greater good."

"This sounds a little too easy," I huffed. "A bit of a fairy tale if you ask me! What about hard work? My father always said that in order to make it in life, You have to work hard, and this certainly doesn't sound too hard to do. Did he know you were going to tell me this before he asked you to help me?"

Gabe laughed. "He knows it now."

"Very funny," I replied sarcastically.

"You're right, Sam; it's very easy, yet it's the hardest thing to do and understand. That's because we were all conditioned to believe that in order to live a comfortable life, we must work hard. Ironically, this is the very thing that robs most people of their true potential and happiness."

"Hmmm... How so? It doesn't make sense. Things don't just create themselves, we must work to create them; it's called being in control. Even I know this," I said.

"Allow me to share a little secret with you, Sam."

"Please do," I said enthusiastically.

"It's the need to control everything that sends your life out of control and into chaos," he said with a chuckle.

"Excuse me!?" I exclaimed.

"Let go of the need to control your life and you'll gain control of your life," Gabe explained, smiling.

"Sorry, Gabe, but that just doesn't add up!" I protested. "It's like saying, 'let go of the wheel and your car will take you where you want to go.'"

Gabe laughed. "If you want to bring cars into it, let me say it this way. Do you think you have control of your car? You may be holding the wheel but your conscious mind isn't constantly thinking about when to turn it or holding down the clutch pedal to change gears, accelerating, decelerating, breaking, and maybe even changing the radio station. You could be having a conversation with someone on your phone or in deep thought, yet you're driving without any effort and without consciously thinking about it. That's because your subconscious has taken over! Your subconscious is in control, even though you think you're in control. In essence, you've inadvertently surrendered control to your subconscious. In life, however, you're reluctant to surrender control to your subconscious and keep trying to figure things out with the limited resources of the conscious mind. Surrender control is life's simple formula, yet it's the hardest thing for a human to do."

I sat there quietly for a moment, thinking about this profound idea Gabe just gave me that I'm not really in control of my life and that my subconscious should be.

"You mean to tell me that I should just let my subconscious take over? Isn't that what crazy people do?" I said defensively.

Gabe laughed, shook his head, and looked directly at me. "What do you think controls your body, Sam? Your body is the vehicle of your soul. Do you consciously think about every breath you take or every other bodily function you need to live? No, the subconscious does it all without you having to think about it. And the body was designed by the master engineer, the Universe!"

"The Universe?!" I asked surprised.

"Yes the Universe, Sam. It's the most intelligent engineer there is. Besides the body, look at nature, childbirth, the seasons! Everything was designed with the highest of intelligence and utmost accuracy. Everything has a purpose and everything has its place and timing. Nothing rushes and nothing worries. Your life was designed by the same engineer. It gave you a purpose and the tools to find it, and all you have to do is let the subconscious take over, and it's very important that you do."

"Wow!" I retorted. "This sounds urgent, Gabe."

"It is!" Gabe replied. "Every day that you're not living your purpose is a day of struggle. You go against the flow. You try to control everything, until you exhaust yourself. Your life isn't about building and engineering your life. Your life is about unravelling what's already there for you."

"Believe me, Gabe, if finding my purpose will make me happy, then I'm all for it! It's not exactly my choice to be unhappy, but, unfortunately, my work and my living conditions keep reminding me of this every day. However, if there's another way, then I'm more than eager to hear it. So what is it?!" I asked impatiently.

"It's not 'what'; it's 'how.'" Gabe teased.

"Okay! How!?"

"Well, Sam, I'm more than happy to tell you, but I'm pretty sure you're going to run for the hills," Gabe kept teasing.

"Try me!" I demanded.

"Okay, here goes!" Gabe announced... Ready!?"

I nodded impatiently.

"Just BE!" Gabe exclaimed and clicked his fingers. "And preferably in the present moment," he added.

"What!? That's it!?" I protested. "BE!?... All that talk about destiny and purpose, and that's all you're giving me? Just BE—"

"And in the present moment..." Gabe interrupted.

"I thought you were going to give me some mantra to chant three times a day or something magical like that, which would transform my life, but 'Be'? What does it even mean!?"

"It's simple, Sam! It means living in the moment and being okay with whatever happens without judging it or categorizing it."

"Not sure I follow you, Gabe."

"Okay, let me put this to you in a different way. Imagine you're in a canoe, travelling downstream. You sit in the canoe, with the paddle in your hands. Do you keep paddling while the canoe is being carried by the stream?" Gabe asked.

"Probably not," I replied.

"Why not?" Gabe asked.

"Because the stream is carrying me already; there's no need to add more effort," I said with conviction.

"When will you use the paddle then?" Gabe asked.

I thought for a second and said, "I imagine I'd use it when I needed to make adjustments, like when the canoe is heading in the wrong direction or when the current is too weak to push me forward."

Gabe nodded in agreement and said, "When you're sitting in the canoe while being carried down the stream, you're 'Being.' You let go of control, sit still, and release all resistance. And when you use the paddle to make adjustments, you're 'responding' to a need to take action."

"Ookkayy," I said suspiciously, "And?"

"Life is the stream, and it will carry you through it effortlessly, if you just 'Be' and let it do its thing, just like a stream carries you in a canoe. When the need arises for you to 'respond,' you'll know with the same certainty as when you know you need to make adjustments with the paddle. That way, you're at peace, knowing that you are where you need to be, without worries or anxiety that you might be heading in the wrong direction. This is BEING. Now you understand?"

"Sounds easy enough," I said.

"Yet it's so hard to do," Gabe said,

"Hmm... I can't see why it would be so hard," I said with scepticism.

Gabe smiled, raised one eyebrow, and said, "It's hard, because the ego keeps nagging you to take control, to do something, to make things happen, until you stop trusting the stream to carry you, and instead, start fighting it, and try to take control, and sometimes you even fight against the current and try to row upstream. Can you imagine how hard it would be to paddle upstream, Sam? Most people expend a lot of energy rowing in the wrong direction mainly due to identification with the ego.

"I can't imagine anyone doing it, unless they want to exhaust themselves. It would be silly," I said.

"Yet they do it with their lives," Gabe replied. "The stream is the sequence of life events that occur. They can either resist them and try to row against the current or gently go with the flow. Sometimes, they go through rapids or over waterfalls and it can be frightening or exciting, depending on whether they resist it or accept it. Life will carry you down your path, Sam, and it will do so a lot easier if you move out of the way. When the time comes for you to act on something, you'll know. The main thing is, don't try to analyze the meaning of everything, just know that whatever happens to you is what needs to happen," said Gabe.

"Wow!" I exclaimed. "I wish my life were that easy."

"Your life seems uneasy because you give everything a meaning and rush to assume that something is broken and you need to take control of the situation. You live in poverty, you collect garbage, and you see yourself as being a failure. This was the meaning you gave it, and that meaning creates a feeling, usually of uncertainty, which leads to depression and anxiety. You then try to correct what you think is broken, even though, in the grand scheme of things, nothing is broken but your perception. Not only is it not broken, but it's a necessary steppingstone. If you, instead, just trust that this is where you need to be right now, you'll just be okay with everything because you'd know that it's only a steppingstone in your path. It's not bad luck, bad karma, or God conspiring against you because you've been a bad boy. It's simply what your path looks like right now. A mountain climber doesn't deem the whole adventure of reaching the top as failure because he encountered a big boulder that blocks his path. The climber will simply see it as an obstacle that he must overcome in order to reach the summit, and he focuses on that task alone, knowing the road continues past the boulder. If he's discouraged, his adventure ends."

"Fair comment," I said. "But it's not easy to look at my situation and just accept that it's okay. Particularly when, every day, I feel the pain of my situation. I lose sleep and have anxiety attacks, and here you are, telling me to do nothing and just accept it?"

"I also said 'In the present moment,'" Gabe reminded. "Be in the moment; that's the other part. The reason you lose sleep and have anxiety attacks is because you let your mind drift into the future and sometimes into the past. If you look at the nature of your anxieties, you'll notice that they come from 'what if' assumptions. Most of the time, you're painting situations in your mind that never happen and probably never will, and you feel anxious about them. You're yelling, 'Ouch!' and feeling the pain of hammering your thumb before you even grab the hammer. Not a very pleasant way to live, Sam."

I stood there, thinking about what Gabe said. It was getting late, I hadn't had lunch, and I was supposed to be at the gym in an hour, but I was mesmerised by what Gabe told me so far. It just resonated with me. Usually, I would dismiss all that new age mumbo jumbo and Joshua's positive thinking spiel, but this was different. It actually made me feel light in my heart; it was almost like instant hope. But the other side of me, probably the ego, kept reminding me that I was speaking to a beggar, albeit, the ex CEO of the largest Chemical company in the world, so he can't be that delusional. I still couldn't get my head around this 'riches to rags' idea, and the idea that my father asked him to look after me. But I guess, for now, I'll take a leaf out of his book and not give it a meaning. Nonetheless, I decided to stick around for a little while longer, and skip the gym, but I was also a little hungry.

"Hey, are you hungry?" I asked Gabe. "I can go and get a couple of hotdogs from Joe's if you like."

"I'm okay, Sam, thank you!" he said cheerfully.

"Are you okay!?" I asked surprised. "Aren't you supposed to be hungry? Or are you a beggar on a diet?"

"I had a big breakfast," he replied.

"You had a big breakfast?!" I asked, surprised. "Even I haven't had a big breakfast, and I have a little money, and you, with no money, already had a big breakfast?!" I laughed.

"I told you, Sam, everything I need comes when I need it. When I'm hungry, the food comes to me somehow. But you go ahead; don't let me hold you back."

"It's okay," I said. "I'm not feeling overly hungry anyway." Of course, I lied. I was famished and drooling over the thought of a Joe hotdog.

"You must have developed an interest in what I'm saying to the point of giving up 'a Joe hotdog,'" Gabe said, laughing.

"It's true," I said. "Something about what you're saying resonates with me for some reason. But I'm not going to lie to you and say that my life is completely changed. I still have to go back to my derelict apartment, I still have to listen to my neighbor's yelling and arguing, I still have to face my landlord's persistent rent collection, and I still have to go to work tomorrow in garbage. Most importantly, I'm still going to feel lonely and handle it all on my own. That's the reality I'm facing."

Gabe looked at me with compassionate eyes and said, "The temporary circumstances you're facing, and I stress 'temporary,' are there for a reason, and they're specifically tailored for you, Sam. You're being 'trained' for the next stage of your path. This wouldn't have happened, had you not been able to handle it. Your soul put them in place, and it's all part of the plan, including the strength to handle them. Nothing is random. The main thing is, again, to not try and give them a meaning or second guess them, and, most importantly, to not attach 'what if' stories to them."

"My soul put these in place?!" I asked with scepticism. "How can that be?"

"Yes, Sam. Your soul is an energy that never dies; it reincarnates into a new body when you die, and prior to reincarnation, it chooses the

74

type of experiences you will have in the physical world. This includes those situations that you perceive as bad. Your soul put these in place, and it knows why. This is why the significant events of your life are already predetermined as I said before. If you look back at some of the significant events in your life, whether you perceive them as good or bad, you'll notice that they occurred seemingly out of the blue, out of your control, and without you even thinking about them or 'requesting' them. These are the predetermined events. Knowing this will make you not judge them and will strengthen the level of trust you have in them."

"So am I basically a soul? Is that what you're saying?" I asked.

"You're a soul having a physical experience. Your physical body is simply the canoe or the car for your soul. Think about it for a second. There are two parts to you. There's the physical part, and there's a mental part. The physical part, which is the mechanical part, is what moves your legs and arms, and other parts of your physical body that you can see and control to your liking or as needed. Are you with me so far?"

"Yes, I'm with you," I said impatiently. "Carry on!"

"Then, there's the mental part, which is really your spiritual part. This part not only allows you to think but also lets you know what you are thinking and understand what you are thinking and why. Every day, you're feeling different emotions that are triggered by something. You might see something that would trigger sadness, happiness, or fear, but it's not the physical part that's feeling it. Although, in some cases, a feeling can result in physical pain, but it's the spiritual side of you that's feeling it. And the thing that lets you know you're feeling it and even lets you know why you're feeling it is called, your 'consciousness.' That consciousness stems from your soul and is tainted by your ego. The only difference is, thoughts that stem from the ego don't feel too good because they clash against your soul's direction," Gabe explained.

"Wow! My physics teacher never told us that," I said, laughing.

"They weren't told that either," Gabe said. "Remember... your Physics teacher is a conveyor of information not a researcher. The main thing to remember, Sam, is that your soul is in command of this canoe, but your ego is trying to sink it. Your body is just a vessel for carrying the soul, but ultimately, it's the soul that gives you your life."

"So, you're saying that the body isn't important? I bust my butt for hours at the gym," I said, laughing.

"Working out will provide your soul with a fit and healthy vessel, and that's important. But a body without a soul is like a canoe without a paddler. Pretty useless."

"Yeah, but in all fairness, the soul wouldn't get anywhere without the body. It would be up the creek without a paddle or a canoe even," I said, laughing. "They both need each other."

"They do," Gabe replied. "But your soul is using your physical body as a vessel to express itself and to experience the journey it came here to experience, and this journey, is already predetermined. Let me put this to you in another way. If you're in a hot desert, you need water to survive, so you carry some water in a canteen. The canteen holds the water, but the water is what's going to keep you alive. Without the water, the canteen would be useless, and you'd die of thirst. The water is what gives the canteen its usefulness. Same with your physical body. It's the soul that gives the physical body its usefulness. The body allows you to perform physical tasks, but before you can perform these tasks, the body first needs to receive instructions from your consciousness. Your thoughts are what make your physical body respond. If you think, *I need to go to the store*, this thought makes your legs move. If you see a beggar, and think, *What a poor beggar; I want to help him,* this thought makes you move your hand inside your pocket. Easy!"

"So let's see if I understand it right," I said tentatively. "When I'm 'BEING,' I let the current carry me and let the soul take over. When I'm needed to act, I'll be given a sign, and until then, I should just chill?"

"Bingo!" Gabe exclaimed. "And that's how easy it is."

"Easier said than done," I protested. "I usually feel guilty or, even worse, lazy, if I'm not doing anything."

"Guilt is your ego nagging. Your ego makes you feel guilty when it wants attention, but really, Sam, you didn't come into this world to be constantly busy and on the go. You're a human BEING not a human DOING. You came here to experience various aspects of life first. You were given talents and various interests in order to make your life more vibrant and joyous. For the ego, these talents and interests are useless, unless they produce financial rewards or recognition from others, but for the soul, these are things to enjoy. The way to a happy fulfilled life is to find the balance between 'doing' and 'being.' When you're called for action, act. When you're called for 'chilling' as you called it, chill and enjoy your other talents and interests."

"Okkay…so how do I know that I'm being called for action then?" I asked.

"Ah! The million dollar question," Gabe teased. "The short answer would be that you just know. Have you ever had an idea that just popped into your head and just took over with such force, that you completely forgot what you were doing or thinking about prior to that idea coming in? Or have you ever done something that involved no resistance or doubt, that just felt natural to do? Like collecting cans or something?" Gabe said, laughing.

"Yeah!" I said with enthusiasm. "All the time! But sometimes they're so ridiculous that I just ignore them," I admitted.

"Ah! You ignore them because the ego wants a reason to do it, and it wants to understand the full picture before it's willing to act. You may get a strong feeling that you need to do something, but the ego wants to know why. It rules it as ridiculous or a waste of time and will try to scare you away from it. Unfortunately, sometimes, you listen to it. Then your soul needs to create another way to get your attention, which can prolong the process. If you trust that there's a purpose, even if you don't know what it is or have the smallest idea why, you would just follow your gut and do it. If doing something, however, is an important piece of your destiny, the ego wouldn't have the power to stop you for long, it can only try to sabotage your progress, but the intensity will grow to a point where not doing it will become more painful than doing it. This is your soul winning. Remember, your soul is the captain of this canoe, and the ego is the pirate that's trying to sink it." Gabe winked.

"Well, I had a strong urge to look for you today, and nothing would have stopped me. So was I meant to be here?" I asked.

"It's quite possible, Sam; time will tell. Sometimes, you meet people who are meant to guide you, supposedly by chance. You just happened to be somewhere and talk to the person next to you, who turns out to be someone who can be of great help to you. But here's the magic. Your soul led you to that place and made you want to talk to that person, and their soul led them to where you are and made them want to talk to you. This is fate. Two souls performing roles in a drama, and it brings both of you great joy and benefit. It's never for the benefit of either one; it's always for the benefit of both of you. This is how you recognize a 'fated' encounter." Gabe nodded.

"Why can't it be just sheer luck?" I asked.

"The ego just calls it 'luck,' because it had nothing to do with the creation of this fortunate situation. But luck is an illusion your ego is trying to trick you into believing in because of its limited view and because it wants to protect its position as an important part of your life," said Gabe.

"Wow!" I said surprised. "What happens if I miss a call for action or just ignore it? Does that mean I change my destiny?"

"You also have free will, Sam, and you can ignore the call for action if you wish. But if it's something that's part of your destined path, your soul won't relent; it'll continue to send signs until you get it. If you continue to ignore them, the intensity of the call for action will increase, sometimes, to the point of what you perceive as a disaster or misfortune. But some people hear better when they're in pain," Gabe said, laughing.

"Great!" I said with discontentment. "No pressure!"

"Most times, you'd just do it, Sam, because it either feels right to do or inspiring and fun, or the pull to do it will outweigh the resistance. It's very hard to miss a sign because it'll take over the ego and be too strong to ignore, so don't worry too much." Gabe grinned and winked at me.

I looked at Gabe with worrisome eyes. "If you ask me, Gabe, this is quite scary because, now, I'll just get paranoid that maybe I'm missing a sign or a call for action. I don't want to suffer pain in order to hear it."

Gabe laughed.

"Why are you laughing?" I asked.

"I'm laughing because you're trying to understand this from your logic and your five senses. That logic insists on seeing everything in a tangible form."

"What do you mean?!" I asked.

"You know!" Gabe exclaimed. "Like thinking you don't have a soul unless you see it, or deeming it as hogwash because you can't touch it, but let me try to explain this to you in a logical sense. Imagine you're driving with a GPS; you trust the GPS to call out the turns, and when it does, you don't question it. If you were distracted by something, or you decide not to take the turn by using your free will, the GPS will perform a route recalculation. This route recalculation, will lead you to the same end point, but via a different and, sometimes, longer one, which represents an experience that you'd perceive as painful. But you'll reach your destination nonetheless.

Your soul is the most accurate GPS system for your life, and if you miss a sign, it'll perform a route recalculation for you. This recalculation will continue, until you're on the right road to your destination. You don't need to know how a GPS is built and works in order to trust it; you just do."

"Interesting. I think I get it—"

"And in the present moment, don't forget!" Gabe interrupted. "You receive the signs and calls for action in the present moment. If your mind is too busy wondering about the past or stressing about the future, it can't hear the instructions that are being given in the moment because of too much mind clutter. This makes it more difficult to distinguish between mind chatter and a real sign." Gabe nodded.

"Yeah, that would be me," I admitted. "I'm always worried and, more often than not, find my thoughts deep into the future."

"That would be most people; so don't feel bad," Gabe consoled.

"That's hardly any consolation," I said sarcastically.

"Are you okay at the moment?" Gabe asked. "You have a roof over your head, you have food in your fridge, and, although you don't like your job very much, you still have a job that provides all of these things, do you not?"

"I suppose I'm okay at the moment," I said sheepishly. "But there's always that element of fear that it would end for the worst."

"Let me ask you this, Sam. When you're driving at night and the headlights only reveal a small section of the road, do you worry about not seeing the rest of the road ahead?"

"No, of course not," I scoffed.

"Why not?" Gabe teased. "After all, you can't see the road; it's dark and sometimes scary. Why aren't you worried that the road might end? Or that the road might lead to a big drop off a cliff?"

"Because I trust that if the road was leading to a drop off a cliff, it would be marked as closed and unsafe for use," I answered

"If your ego tried to scare you that the road might end beyond the light, would you get scared? Would you fall for it?" Gabe asked.

"No, of course not. It would be silly. What's your point?" I asked impatiently.

"The point is that when it comes to trusting the road you're on in life, you're afraid that it might lead you to the edge of a cliff, beyond the point you can see the road. And you don't trust that it would give you a warning sign if you were headed toward danger. Why is that?" Gabe continued teasing.

"Hmmm... I see your point," I conceded.

"The point is, Sam, just like you trust that the road still exists beyond the reach of the headlights, even though you cannot see it, so you should trust that your path still leads you to where you need to go, despite not being able to see beyond the present moment. This will eliminate any fear of the unseen and unknown. It will free your mind from worrying about things it need not worry about. This is why the present moment is the only thing that truly exists and the only time that truly matters. Anything beyond that point is in the dark area your headlights don't reach and will be revealed as you continue to move forward. "

"What you're teaching me is amazing, Gabe! In fact, I'm surprised that you're not sharing your wisdom with the rest of the world through seminars and workshops. It would probably make you a lot more money than what you collect as a beggar," I joked.

"What's wrong with sharing it as a beggar?" Gabe asked.

"Well, I'd assume that most people would be more open to such teaching if it came from the former CEO of T.R Chem than from a beggar. I mean, I had my doubts when I met you. Just look at how people stare at us; almost every person who walks by turns their head and frowns, wondering why I'm talking to a beggar."

Gage laughed. "But you're still here, Sam, listening to me. Are you not?"

"Yes, but to be honest, it's probably because you said that my father asked you to help me, and that CEO thing made me see you in a different light. You're right; we do tend to judge by appearances, don't we?"

"When you look beyond appearances, you're stepping outside the realm of the ego and you're listening from your soul. That's why I've chosen to become a beggar; I needed you to listen from your soul." Gabe smiled.

"I hear you, Gabe," I said softly.

"Well, I'm glad you stayed, Sam; your father would be proud." Gabe smiled.

"Yeah, me too," I said. "I'm growing quite fond of you, I must admit." I laughed.

Chapter 5

There's Nothing to Manifest

As the day stretched into the afternoon, I continued sitting under the tree, listening to Gabe the beggar talk about life. I had so many questions.

"I remember as a child, my mother used to tell me all the time that I could have anything I wanted if I only believed I could have it, that nothing was off limits, and that God only wanted the best for me. But she ended up leaving me, and my father ended up dead. How can I believe that God wants the best for me after he took my parents away from me and put me in a position of struggle and desperation? I was always told that it's up to me to manifest my reality. People kept telling me to be positive, think positive; otherwise, bad things will manifest. This notion scared me; it scared me a lot," I said.

"Why is it scary, Sam?" Gabe asked.

"It's scary because I don't want bad things to happen. I would often find myself fighting with my negative thoughts, telling them to go away, so I don't accidentally manifest them," I said tremulously.

"Good and bad are just a system of judgment your ego uses to make sense of things. If something makes you feel good or if a desired result is realized, it calls it good. If something makes you feel bad or if what you hoped to achieve didn't happen in the way you wanted it to happen, it calls it bad. That's because the ego has a very limited view and can't see the full picture, nor is it interested in seeing the full picture. If your ego were baking a cake, it would have rejected it based on the flavor of the individual ingredients, rather than the flavor of what the combination of the ingredients produces once baked." There's so much more to the story than meets the eye, but when you judge it based on the 'individual ingredients' of the full picture, you also attach a feeling based on the individual ingredient. This causes a lot of unnecessary anguish."

"So are you saying that having negative thoughts won't manifest into negative scenarios?" I asked. "Because I know a lot of people who would disagree with you."

Gabe smiled, nodded, and said, "No more than thinking negative about the road you're driving on will change it or lead you to a different town. If the idea that you can manifest anything you want were true, this world would have been thrown into chaos. Imagine if every employee in my company were able to manifest the position they wanted in the company? Imagine if they all wanted to be managers? The company wouldn't be able to operate with only managers. It needs the secretary to take the calls, it needs the sales personnel to sell the products, it needs the manufacturers to make the

86

products, and it needs the delivery drivers to deliver the products. The company was able to operate successfully because each person had their unique responsibility that contributed to the whole. The universe operates in a precise order and timing. Everything in nature has its unique assignment to accomplish to keep the Universe's wheels in motion, as one might say. If a bee decided one day that it didn't feel like pollinating and making honey, it would have a devastating effect on everything. We too, as humans, each has a unique assignment to follow to keep the order, and not doing it has a devastating effect on everyone and everything."

"I'm quite happy to not try to manifest anything," I admitted with a sense of relief. "It hurts to do that. Constantly fighting with your mind to think in a different direction, trying to block negative thoughts. It hurts! And it's tiring!"

"Then stop hurting yourself," Gabe teased. "You don't need to manifest anything; everything is already in place for you. It's like train stations. The stations are already in place; you don't need to do anything apart from moving forward toward the stations. You only see the stations when you've reached them.

"There are two types of manifestation," Gabe explained. "One type is the manifestation within your intended path. Those who manifest within their intended path have the illusion that they manifested it, but don't realize that the reason they desired something so bad was because it was a part of their intended path. If you remember, one of the ways the soul guides you is by making you feel enthusiastic about something. You then follow your passion for that thing, and because it's something that was meant to happen in your life, you confuse yourself by thinking that it was the thought that manifested that thing you so desperately desired. That initial thought came from your higher self. You were led to it; you didn't create it." Gabe nodded.

"And the other type?" I asked eagerly.

"The other type of manifestation is the type that comes from desperation and fear. It's the type of manifestation that never manifests. People try to manifest big houses, lots of money, and perfect relationships because they lack those things and believe that acquiring them will fill in the gaps that caused that desperation and unhappiness. They want a short cut without having to go through the lessons and experiences in their lives. They want to jump to the position of CEO without the effort of climbing up the ladder and gaining the experience they need to advance into more executive positions. They say 'why can't my soul just lead me to a pot of gold?'" Gabe winked, referring to my earlier rant.

"Very funny! you got me!" I said scornfully. "But I still wouldn't mind walking my path in comfort. I can still learn the lessons, but in comfort."

Gabe laughed and said, "Struggle and desperation teach you a different lesson than the one you learn from a comfortable place, and, sometimes, the lesson or experience must come from a 'desperate' place in order to teach you the right lesson that was designed for you."

"I sure as hell hope that there are some pleasant lessons for me also," I said with slight sarcasm.

"Winter doesn't change its length, no matter how hard you try to extend it or wish it to be shorter. What needs to happen in your life, Sam, will happen whether you are consciously thinking it or not. The only question is, do you want to walk your path in joy or in fear and anxiety? Either way, you'll get to the finish line."

"Hmm… Of course, I'd rather walk my path in joy," I said with conviction. "But it's not always up to me. Stuff happens, you know."

"Yeah... stuff happens," Gabe repeated. "A man is driving down the highway and has a blowout….stuff happens…. He's upset, angry, and frustrated, but has no idea that had this blowout not happened, he would have been killed in a head-on collision with a massive truck. Your ego, with its limited capacity, ruled it as outright 'bad,' but your soul, with its panoramic view, saw it as a blessing. There's no telling the reasons why stuff happens, Sam; there's only the trust that they happen for us, not to us. There's a huge difference you know! So if you'd rather walk your path in joy, just BE! Sit in the canoe and enjoy the ride because that's all life is, a ride, and you're guided every step of the way. However, you must play by the rules, one of which is that you do your part and your part only, and if you interfere with the rules, and try to control areas that aren't for you to control, you're interrupting a sacred flow, and the consequence is an undesired result, which leads to disappointment, fear, and uncertainty. Remember, disappointment can only stem from expectations. If you have no expectations, you'll have no disappointments, only surprises." Gabe nodded and smirked.

"Yeah, uncertainty is my middle name," I muttered.

Gabe laughed. "You're not alone there, Sam."

"What about love?" I asked.

"What about it?" Gabe asked back.

"Will I ever find it? Or is being alone and lonely a part of my destiny also?

"Alone? Or lonely?" Gabe asked.

"What's the difference?" I said with a cocky tone.

"Oh... there's a big difference, Sam. Alone is a state of being all one. Lonely is a feeling of separation. To be alone can benefit you greatly at times, and it's not unusual for your soul to want you to be alone at times. There are lessons and self-realizations that can only be accomplished and achieved while you're alone. Some things require you to avoid outside influences and distractions in order to complete them. Lonely, however, is a feeling that derives from your ego. It's a pack mentality. It's the feeling you have when you falsely think that you need people in your life all the time, or that you must belong in a group, in order to have a sense of self-worth and to feel that you're desirable," Gabe explained.

"Hmm... Interesting way of looking at it," I said. "But there's nothing wrong with wanting to be with a special person, a soul mate who I can share myself with and express the feeling of love."

Gabe smiled and asked, "Are you ready for a soul mate, Sam? Are you able to share yourself with someone right now?"

"Hmm... Good question," I said. "I'm not sure. How do I know?"

"Just like trying to manifest something out of desperation, won't manifest good results, if any, so wanting to be with someone out of desperation won't work, or it will attract an incompatible partner. If you're desperate to be with someone just because you're feeling lonely and bored or you feel that time is against you and you must hurry before you're too old, you're in danger of settling on the first person who shows an inkling of interest in you, rather than being with someone who is suitable for you. It's taking a turn against your GPSs programmed path, but it also carries the possibility of inharmonious existence, pain, and the danger of growing apart because each soul will always push in the direction they were meant to go, and there's no escaping this. This is the reason why anyone who gives up or compromises a fundamental part of their soul in order to accommodate a partner will always end up chasing it back into their lives," Gabe said.

I looked at Gabe with a squint in my eyes, "How do I know if someone is suitable? Should I prepare a questionnaire and tick the boxes? 'Ahhh, do you like spaghetti?'" I laughed.

Gabe smiled and nodded. "Well Sam, in order to prepare the questionnaire, you'd have to know yourself, wouldn't you? Do you know yourself well enough to know what suits you and what doesn't? Because if all you need is someone who likes spaghetti, then you shouldn't be single right now, or ever, for that matter."

"Hmm… I think I do," I replied tentatively. "I mean… I do long to hold someone sometimes. I think I can make someone happy."

"I'm sure you will someday, Sam," said Gabe with a soft compassionate voice…." But remember, meeting someone is easy. Growing with someone is a different story all together. Who you are now is going to change as you mature and experience more of life. Your soul knows you better than you do, and it knows who you would become long before you do, and it will signal to you when you meet its match," said Gabe with conviction.

"Will it really!? Can I really trust that?!" I asked, surprised, while feeling a sense of relief at the same time.

"Just as much as you trust the GPS," Gabe said, laughing. "Why aren't you approaching that waitress?"

"Selena?!" I replied, surprised. "You know about Selena?!"

"I move around a lot, Sam. I've seen you at Frank's Diner; I've seen the way you look at her."

"Yeah, that obvious, huh? I guess I'm a little intimidated by her. I don't have the courage to tell her what I do and where I live," I said sheepishly. "In fact, this is the reason I never pursued any woman, even when it was obvious that they were interested in me."

"What you do Sam is make an honest living. Where you live, has nothing to do with what you are. You decided that Selena wants someone rich based on your ego's outlook on life. Would you rather someone love you for what you have or your status? Or would you rather someone love you unconditionally for what you are inside? I can tell you from my experience as a wealthy man that I never had the experience of true love. True love comes from the inside out, not from the outside in. Maybe this is the lesson you're here to learn. To help you set yourself free from this delusional assumption, and make you more confident in yourself, and more receptive to recognizing your soul mate."

"Well, I still don't find the courage to approach her. I still freeze when I see her. I guess you're right when you said that we have been conditioned to think that we value our worth by how much money we have, the type of job that we do, and other ego aspects. I can see it now, and I can see how deeply rooted within our psyche it is to the point that, even though I understand it and I can see it now, it still scares me. It's not easy to shake off, is it?" I said.

Gabe laughed and said, "Sam, what's the worst that could happen?"

I thought for a second. "Hmm... she says no, I guess."

"And what's the issue with her saying no?" Gabe kept challenging.

"No issue, apart from feeling rejected, and the embarrassment that follows," I admitted.

"Ah! The embarrassment!" Gabe chuckled. "The ego hates rejections, doesn't it? It sees it as 'you're not good enough,' 'You're not worthy,' 'something's wrong with you.' But really, all that person rejected was your request for a date. They don't know you well enough to reject anything else, and if they did know you, you'd know whether or not you have a connection."

"I think I have a connection with Selena," I said with slight doubt. "I mean, she's always nice to me and always friendly. She seems to give me extra attention. I always look back after I leave the diner, to see if she'd give me a second look, and she always does."

"Sam, she is a waitress; it's her job to be friendly," Gabe said.

"Great! Thanks for the confirmation," I said dejectedly.

"Sam, if Selena were meant to be a part of your destiny, you would find the courage and the right moment to ask her. Your soul would make sure of that. The beauty about kindred souls is that they recognize each other on a soul level, and the attraction is mutual and beyond the ego. If she isn't a part of your destiny, however, than maybe there's a reason why you feel intimidated to ask her out. Maybe your soul is creating this resistance for a reason. That's the beauty of finding your soul mate. When you're with your intended one, the power of the soul easily overpowers the false self, that's because nothing else really matters. This is why you sometimes hear stories about people who say they knew right there and then that they met their soul mate. It was an inner feeling, regardless of outside appearances."

I sat there, trying to take in what Gabe just laid on me, then I gave him a confused look and said, "Wow! We really don't have control over anything."

"Nor should you need to, Sam. Just sit in the canoe," Gabe replied, chuckling. "Sam, all I'm saying is that your soul chose the right partner for you when it planned its journey. Sometimes, it even planned multiple 'temporary' partners to prepare you for your soul mate, to help you get to know yourself and understand yourself and the qualities you need in a partner, in order for you to grow together harmoniously. The question is, are you willing to wait?"

"Sure I am, but I hope I won't have to wait till I'm fifty."

"Again, time and age have nothing to do with it. It all comes down to the social conditioning, which gave you a generic template, dictating that you must do something by a certain age or you'll miss out. It's like dictating that all plants should grow at the same rate. For some, it happens early, but for others, it happens later in life. It all depends on the path your soul has chosen." Gabe smiled.

"I guess that explains why my mother left my father," I said.

"Only your mother knows why, Sam, but she obviously did what she had to do, so try not to judge her too much," said Gabe with a soft voice.

"It's hard not to," I said.

"You're obviously still angry at her, and that's understandable. But you also must understand that you chose your parents for a reason. Your soul was prepared for your mother's sudden departure and for your father's death because that's what it needed for its expression. Your ego, however, will never understand it or give you comfort," said Gabe.

"I doubt I'll ever find comfort in that; I guess I just need to come to terms with it. I can't change the situation anyway," I said morosely.

"Sam, I promise you that, in time, you will understand a lot of things that you can't understand at the moment. Hindsight is a tool we all have, if we use it," said Gabe.

"What's the point in hindsight? It happened anyway and we can't change the past," I replied.

"No, you can't change the past, nor should you want to. Hindsight can help you understand that your life does have a formula. It helps you see how the pieces fit together, and helps you build trust in the process. Unfortunately, you're still young and don't have much data to go by, but as you grow older, you'll have more data to look back to. Patience, son." Gabe smiled.

"Yeah, that patience again!" I said with frustration.

"Yeah, that annoying patience," said Gabe with a cynical tone. "Everybody wants instant gratification. You rush a fruit tree to grow and be ready ahead of time, and you get a tasteless fruit. Patience is simply the understanding that everything has its own time to develop and a life span, and nothing will change that fact. The only thing impatience will give you is a gruelling experience, in which you live in a constant state or wanting and waiting. You're yelling at the tomato plant to grow already because you're hungry now." Gabe couldn't stop laughing.

"I'm glad you're amused!" I said.

"Oh, I'm amused alright," Gabe said, wiping tears from his eyes.

"Anyway, it's getting late; I probably should get going," I said in a soft voice.

"It's been a real pleasure talking to you, Sam," said Gabe with a happy voice.

"Where are you going now? Do you have some place to go to?" I asked.

"Wherever my soul will lead me, Sam. I'm sure it will be exciting," Gabe said.

"Maybe we can talk again," I suggested.

"Maybe, Sam," said Gabe. "But I think I told you everything there is to know in order to live a peaceful, purposeful, worry-free life. It's so simple and so accurate that there's no reason why you shouldn't succeed. Remember, you don't create your life, you unfold it." Gabe clasped his palms together and bowed.

"Yeah, I hope so," I said. "One thing is for sure. You definitely gave me a complete different perspective on life, and, to be honest, as strange as it may seem, it resonates a lot."

"Ahh... resonates!" Gabe exclaimed. "I love it! Resonance is a confirmation from the soul."

"There you go!" I said. "I've been listening."

"Take care of yourself, Sam," Gabe said, smiling.

"Yeah!" I exclaimed. "Well, maybe I'll see you tomorrow? I'll be taking my walk after work," I said with enthusiasm.

"That would be nice, Sam. I'll see you when I'm looking at you," Gabe said, laughing.

"Well, just in case I might have questions or concerns; you know," I said with humorous defensiveness.

"Of course, Sam. But just remember, if it's a question or a concern worth worrying about, then you already have the answers to them inside you. Just sit in the canoe, Sam, and let it come to you." Gabe smiled.

"Oh, that's right! The canoe! Let the stream carry you, and use the paddle when you need to make adjustments."

"You're a good student, Sam; I have a feeling you're going to do very well in your life."

"Thanks!" I said cheerfully. "Anyway, I'll see you…maybe tomorrow?"

Gabe nodded and sat there in a lotus position, watching me walk away. I walked about twenty feet and stopped. I wanted to say thank you to Gabe once again. I turned around.

"Hey, Thanks agai…n…….Gabe!?.....Gabe?!" Gabe was gone. I stood there stunned, calling Gabe again and again. He just vanished like he did at the market. But this time, he had nowhere to go or hide. At least at the market, there was the possibility of him being obscured by the crowd or the stalls, but here in the park? I walked up the footpath, looked between the trees, I even looked up the trees, but there was no sign of him.

I sat there on the grass; my heart was racing like a steam engine. *This can't be!* I thought to myself. *This must be another magic trick. People don't just vanish like that,* I kept mulling in my head.

I sat on the grass for another half hour, trying to bring myself back to my sanity. I had a million thoughts going through my head at once. Did my father ask Gabe to help me from the other side? My heart was still palpitating at an alarming rate and my head was pounding. All I wanted to do was to tell someone so they could confirm that I wasn't crazy, that things like that were normal. But even to me, it didn't seem normal, so how was I going to convince anyone that what just happened was real. Who am I going to tell this to? People would think I'm crazy. Maybe I am crazy. How else can I possibly explain this? Selena! What about Selena? Maybe I can tell her? Oh, God! I can't even tell her what I do, let alone tell her that I spent the whole day with a ghost.

I got up, and started to walk home, feeling a little groggy and disillusioned. "Did I just speak to a ghost?" I muttered to myself, while feeling a shiver throughout my whole body. "I don't believe in ghosts!" I said to myself. "There has to be a logical explanation for this." But I couldn't come up with any. Maybe I can talk to Joshua about this. He's into all that spiritual stuff. I tried to rehash a few different ways to tell this in a way that would make sense even to Joshua, but it all sounded unbelievable and pretty crazy.

The next morning, I went to work, feeling like I just got hit by a truck. After tossing and turning all night and not getting much sleep, I had to garner any ounce of energy I could muster. Today was a big garbage run, and I seriously wasn't up to this big task. I arrived at the depot. Joshua was already there ready to go, when he looked at me and said, "Gee, Sam! Are you okay? You look like you've just seen a ghost!" He laughed. "Another late night?"

I looked at him with confused eyes and said, "Actually, I did see a ghost."

Joshua laughed and said, "Well, you sure have the face to support that. But jokes aside, Sam, we better get started; we have a big run today."

There you have it, I thought to myself. *Of course, he's going to call it a joke. It sounds like a joke.* I stepped on the back of the truck as we started moving toward the starting point of the garbage run. Joshua kept talking loudly over the roar of the truck engine, but his voice and words, just went over my head. My mind was dwelling on one thing, the disappearing beggar, again!

Joshua noticed that I wasn't being my usual self. He kept giving me looks like he noticed something. Eventually, he asked, "Is everything okay, Sam? You're very quiet today. Do you want to talk about it?"

"No, I'm good I guess," I replied with a tired low tone. "Just tired is all," I said.

I really wanted to talk to Joshua about what had happened yesterday with Gabe, but I just couldn't bring myself to even start this kind of conversation. Joshua was the only person I considered a friend, and I was afraid that maybe if I told him, he would deem me a lunatic.

"You picked the worst day to be tired. Let me know if you need help with anything," he said with a chuckle.

"I'll be alright," I said. "The stench will wake me up." I smiled.

To my amazement, I survived the day, considering the turmoil that was wreaking havoc inside of me. Joshua was still a little concerned for me. He definitely could tell there was something wrong with me, and throughout the shift, he kept looking at me with an inquisitive stare, but he didn't pry too much. That's the thing about Joshua; he's never pushy or overly nosey. I guess he thought that a good night sleep was what I needed, but if he only knew what was really going on inside my head. If only I could find the courage to tell him. I wanted to be sure first that what happened to me the previous day, was real and not some delusion that I developed as a result of my increasing depression and anxieties.

I decided to look for Gabe. Last time he disappeared on me, I found him in the park, and this was the first place I went to look for him. This time, I had only one question for him, and I wasn't going to let him beat around the bush like he did last time. I arrived at the park, and walked from end to end, but Gabe was nowhere to be seen. I walked back and forth, from the spot we were at yesterday, back to the public bench he was when I first met him, but he wasn't there. I sat there on the bench and started crying, muttering to myself, "Where are you, Gabe? Where are you?" when a big black and red butterfly suddenly landed on my shoulder, flapping its wings rapidly. There was a sudden sense of calmness in me. The butterfly kept flapping its wings, as if it was consoling me. I turned my head toward the butterfly and said, "Hello little fellow, have you seen Gabe by any chance?" The butterfly didn't seem to be afraid of me; it stood there on my shoulder for a few more seconds, then it flew away.

I felt emotional and overwhelmed. I remember my mother telling me that butterflies are God's messengers. She used to say that when I see a butterfly, it means that God is telling me that it's time for change and transformation. That's what I loved about my mom, she always explained things to me in metaphors and illustrations.

I kept thinking about my father and that maybe there's another dimension where the dead are transported to. Tears kept rolling down my cheeks; everything felt so surreal. I was trying to draw a line between fact and fiction. I know Gabe was real; I know our conversation was real. Everything Gabe said yesterday was still clear in my head. Every word he spoke was still clear in my head. But at

101

what point does it become fiction? Did he really know my father? Or did he mean he knows him from the other side?

If it's true and Gabe came from the other side… "Okay, stop, stop!" I commanded myself, "This is crazy! Don't even go there; this isn't a possibility you can entertain."

I wiped the tears off my face, got up, and started walking back home. I felt exhausted and needed to get some sleep and rest my mind, or I would have to admit myself to the mental ward. *I'll try looking for him again tomorrow,* I thought to myself. I have to find him; I have to get to the bottom of this, again.

Chapter 6

Joshua to the Rescue.

After three weeks of looking for Gabe every day and everywhere to no avail, I decided to give up on him. I couldn't continue spending my time on this. Obviously, I was a victim of some lonely beggar who gets a kick out of telling stories to unsuspecting, vulnerable people like me. "Yeah, right! CEO my butt," I muttered; although, I had to admit, the two times he pulled those disappearing acts were pretty impressive. Maybe he was just a quick runner, I thought to myself, trying to rationalize it with some sort of natural explanation. Suddenly, the idea popped into my head to Google Gabriel Taylor and see a picture of him on the Internet. It would confirm whether or not the beggar was Gabriel Taylor or a fraud, and I could move on with my life.

I ran straight to the library, which had a computer with free Internet. I was a man on a very important mission. I entered the library, looking a little frazzled and breathing heavily after my run, and walked toward one of the booths with a computer. Still breathing heavily, I typed in T. R. Chem Gabriel Taylor CEO, selected Images, and clicked the search icon. The computer was slow and took several seconds to load the search results. Sweat dripped on the keyboard as I impatiently urged it to hurry. "Come on! Come on!" I commanded the computer. The search results finished loading and there he was in the first row of pictures, Gabe the beggar. His eyes were brown and his face was clean-shaven but it was him; it was the beggar who just appeared into my life from out of nowhere. The beggar my father had sent to look after me. So Gabe really was Gabriel Taylor, ex CEO of T. R. Chem. I clicked on the picture and then clicked on the page it came from, a Wikipedia page about him. Under the picture on Wikipedia, it said, "Born: Gabriel Charles Taylor, May 26, 1943, Fairfield, Iowa. Died, June 11, 1988 (aged 45), Los Angeles, California. Cause of death: Suicide."

I sat there staring at the screen, looking directly into his eyes and rereading the facts about his death, and I started sobbing like a baby. The woman sitting next to me asked, "Are you okay? Is everything alright?" I turned to her and nodded. Tears were rolling down my face. She looked at the screen and asked, "Did you know this man?" I nodded slowly in confirmation, but I couldn't speak, as I was still too emotional and choking back the sobs. I stood up, wiped my tears with my sleeve, and left the library.

I stood there at the top of the wide circular front stairs of the library. I looked up to the sky and whispered, "Thank you, Gabe" as I felt the wind blowing gently in the back of my neck. I walked slowly down the wide steps, and just sat at the bottom of the stairs. Suddenly, the black and red butterfly landed on my shoulder again, flapping its wings rapidly as it did in the park. I turned toward the butterfly and

104

tried to stroke it gently with my finger. The butterfly jumped on my finger, showing no fear of me. I lowered my hand with the butterfly still on my finger, and said softly, "You know Gabe, don't you?" The butterfly flapped its wings again and flew off. I watched it disappear into the distance. Tears were rolling down my face. I felt that the butterfly was a messenger from heaven. Maybe my father was watching over me and sent Gabe to look after me. Gabe was right; I was reaching a point from which there was no return because I had made the decision to end my life the day I met Gabe, but now I have no desire to give up on life. Maybe I was going through personal transformation. I looked up to the blue sky again and whispered, "I'm okay, Dad; I'm okay."

I stood up and started walking toward Joshua's house, which wasn't far from the library. I had to talk to him, now that I knew that I hadn't been hallucinating or tricked. I felt so overwhelmed by this whole experience, I just couldn't hold it in any more, I couldn't keep it to myself anymore; I had to let it out. I had to share it with someone, and I felt that Joshua was the right person to talk to about this. He would definitely understand or at least help me make sense of it all. I was still quite emotional and teary; I felt a slight tremble throughout my body as I walked slowly toward Joshua's street. My head was bent toward the ground as I kept rehashing the words Gabe spoke to me, remembering his soft voice and chuckles. I thought about his hypnotic fluorescent blue eyes that gave me a sense of calmness whenever he was looking into my eyes. I guess I missed him and wished I could see him again. But maybe his job was done, or maybe he moved on to the next person who was contemplating suicide. Maybe this was what my mother meant when she said that there were angels among us who helped us and protected us. I kept walking slowly with my head still down when a voice to my right said, "Do you have a couple of dollars, son?"

My heart skipped a beat; I stopped and turned toward the voice, and down on the ground, on a piece of cardboard, sat a beggar. He was wearing dirty clothes, his hands were covered with dirt, and he was leaning on a big sack that contained his belongings. I looked at the beggar straight in the eyes as he extended his arm with his palm open, hoping that I would put some money in his hand. I smiled and said, "Yes, I do." I reached into my pocket, pulled out ten dollars, and placed it in his hand. "Here you go, my friend; I'm sorry, but that's all I have," I said softly.

"Oh... God bless!... God bless!" he said excitedly. His eyes were lit up with excitement like a kid in a candy shop. I nodded and kept walking then turned around to look at the beggar again. The beggar clenched his fist with the money in it as if it were the most precious thing to him. He looked at me again, and gave me a big smile with wide-open eyes. I smiled back and kept walking. I realized how such a small act of kindness could brighten up the day of even the most unfortunate. How important it is to be kind to those who don't have much. It made me think about the day Gabe asked me if I had a couple of dollars, and I replied with scorn, refusing to give it to him. I was looking down on him simply because of his appearance. I felt sad, thinking about how cruel and judgmental we can be toward those who don't have much. We sometimes forget that there are less fortunate people out there who rely on our care and empathy, but we pass them by because we're so disconnected from each other and are just busy taking care of our own selves, and surviving. This beggar had nothing, but he still made the effort to smile and show appreciation for something so small. It made me feel love inside, knowing that I had made a difference in a stranger's life, even if were only for one minute. It made me realize that he didn't just receive ten dollars from me; he also received a message of love. He now knows that I care; he knows somebody cares. Maybe Gabe wasn't joking; maybe a beggar's purpose really is to give us an opportunity to express generosity and practice the act of giving.

I turned onto the street where Joshua lives and walked toward his house. I unlatched the small picket gate in front of his house, and walked up to the front door. I could hear Billie Holiday playing from inside his house. *Such a lovely voice* I thought. My mother used to play her music all the time, and hearing it now, made me more emotional and nostalgic. I pushed the doorbell and waited.

The door opened, and Joshua's wife Louisa peered out through the screen door. "Oh, hello, Sam! Come in!" she said cheerfully, and opened the door to let me in.

"Hi, Mrs. Jackson. I'm sorry to drop in like this, unannounced, but there's something I need to speak with Joshua about," I said with a soft apologetic voice.

"Not a problem at all; you're always welcome here, Sam. Joshua's in the shed; I'll take you to him," she said with smiling eyes and a loving embrace.

Louisa noticed some signs of upset on my face, as she ushered me in. "Is everything alright, Sam?" she asked with a concerned tone.

"I'm not sure," I replied. "That's why I need Joshua." I smiled.

"Well, he'll be happy to see you; come with me," she said kindly.

Billie Holiday was still playing. "Nice music," I commented.

Louisa looked at me with a smile and said, "Billie Holiday, she's my favorite. Do you know Billie Holiday?"

"My mother used to play her all the time, particularly when she had a hard time, she would always sit on the porch and just rock on the chair and listen to Billie Holiday with her eyes closed," I said with a tone filled with longing.

"I bet you miss her," Louisa said sympathetically.

"Yes I do," I replied softly.

Louisa opened the screen door at the back of the house and yelled to Joshua, that I was there to see him.

Joshua stepped out of the shed, holding a towel and wiping his hands.

"Hey, Sam, ma boy! What brings you to this neck of the woods?" he asked with cheer in his voice.

"Well, there's something I need to talk to you about. I mean, I've been trying to make sense of it for three weeks now, and I think I'm stuck between two worlds. At first, I was embarrassed to talk about it, because I was certain that you'd laugh at me, but now, I'm starting to believe that maybe it's real, maybe I'm not crazy, maybe I'm—"

"It's the beggar, isn't it?" Joshua interrupted.

"Yes, it is," I said quietly. "How did you know?!"

"I see!" said Joshua with a compassionate voice. "Come into the shed, Sam; we'll have a chat."

We walked into the shed. Joshua got a couple of Dr. Peppers from his small bar fridge he had stacked under his workbench, cracked them open, and handed one to me.

"Thanks!" I said. "I could do with one of these."

"Cheers!" Joshua said and clinked his bottle against mine.

I looked around the shed, Joshua had dozens of different tools hanging neatly on the walls around the shed. "What are you making?" I asked.

Joshua pointed at a wooden square on the workbench with his bottle. "I'm making a cabinet for the television."

"Nice!" I joked. "It's important to keep the TV comfortable and cosy."

Joshua laughed. "Yeah, I like making all sorts of useless stuff, but, in truth, this is my creative time; it's my meditation. It keeps me in the present moment: just me, my tools, and my creations. Helps me clear my head. I also like wood carving." Joshua picked up a wooden figurine of a woman's torso and showed it to me.

"Wow, Josh! This is awesome! I didn't know you could do that?" I said, surprised. "I wish I could do it."

"I didn't know I could do it either until I tried," he said. "I once saw this guy on TV who makes them and sells them at markets, and I was immediately hooked on it. I felt an immense desire to do it, so I went and bought some carving tools and some blocks of pine wood, and within a few days, I was making them. As it turned out, I was quite good at it. There are a few around the house." He took a swig of his soda.

"Wow!" I replied. "You should sell them. Maybe you'd be able to quit the garbage job if it does well."

"Nah!" Joshua objected. "I just enjoy making them for myself; I have no desire to kill the fun by adding business pressure and deadlines. When I do wood carving, I immerse myself in it; I take my time and enjoy the process of making them. It helps me shut out the outside world. It's very relaxing. I don't have to finish them in a certain time; I take my time with them."

"Fair enough," I said. "It's just that they're so beautiful; I'm sure someone would want to give you money for them."

Joshua smiled. "Thanks, Sam, but sometimes a hobby is just a hobby. Besides, I like the garbage job." He let loose with a big belly laugh.

The shed door opened and Louisa came in with a tray of sandwiches.

"I made you boys some sandwiches," she said cheerfully.

"Thank you, Mrs. Jackson," I said excitedly.

"Please Sam, call me Louisa. All that Mrs. business makes me feel like a principal in a boarding school." She laughed and handed me a sandwich on a napkin.

"Thank you, Louisa!" I said. "I'm starving! I gave my lunch money to a beggar on the way here."

"That's very generous, Sam," said Louisa, impressed by the gesture. "And, as you can see, what goes around, comes around." She smiled.

"Yeah, it felt good too," I said proudly. "You should have seen his eyes when I handed him ten dollars. It was like it was the most amount of money he had ever seen."

"Now that's noble!" Joshua emphasized. "Giving when you have plenty is easy, but giving when you don't have much, that's true love." He took a bite of his sandwich and added, laughing, "Besides, a sandwich like this you couldn't buy anywhere."

"Yeah, it's delicious, wow!" I said and devoured the sandwich almost in seconds.

Joshua looked at his wife and said, "Sam had a very mysterious encounter with a beggar a while back." he emphasized *mysterious*, hinting that his wife should know what it means. "And he came out of nowhere." Joshua nodded and winked at his wife.

Louisa looked at me then at Joshua. "Aha... I see," she said sombrely. "Well, I'll leave you boys to it." She smiled and walked out of the shed, closing the door behind her, while staring me in the eyes as though she were concerned about something.

"What was that all about?" I asked Joshua.

Joshua pulled up a couple of bar stools, placed one in front of me, and sat on the other.

"So, Sam, what's happening with the beggar?" he asked

111

I sat on the stool, took a swig of my soda, and said, "I'm not sure how to say it without sounding crazy."

Joshua smiled. "Try me!"

"Okay." I took a deep breath and exhaled sharply… "Do you remember when I told you about the beggar who knew my name and said he knew me?" I asked.

"The one who kept you awake?" Joshua said cheekily.

"Yeah, that one!" I answered with conviction. "The day I told you about him, I went to the market to pick up some groceries, and, in the crowd, there he was again, staring directly at me."

I walked toward him, to find out why he was there looking at me, but, by the time I got to him, he was gone. At first, I thought he dodged me somehow through the crowd, but the area was fenced off, and there was nowhere for him to go.
The next day, I decided to go looking for him, because this disappearing act kept me awake at night, as you know. I couldn't stop thinking about it. So I went back to the park, where I first met him, and had a pretty interesting conversation with him. It changed my whole perspective on life. But then, the most unbelievable thing happened—"

"He just vanished," Joshua interrupted half way through my sentence.

"Yeah!" I said surprised. "How did you know? This was the part I was a little afraid to tell you. He literally vanished without a trace, like he was a wizard or something. Sounds crazy, doesn't it!? Do you think I was hallucinating?" I asked Joshua with slight concern.

"I don't think you were, Sam," he said with a sympathizing tone.

"Really!? You believe me!?" I asked with a tone of relief.

Joshua walked to the bar fridge, grabbed two more Dr. Peppers, cracked them open, and handed me another bottle. "Here, Sam, I think you're going to need it," he said, smiling.

"Why? What's going on?!" I asked, concerned. "Not that I mind having another soda, but you sound a little dramatic."

"Let me tell you a little story that's happened around twenty years ago," Joshua said.

"Okay... I'm listening," I said, intrigued.

"This goes back to the summer of 1998. I was a young man about your age, and I was lost, angry, and confused. Very similar to you, Sam. I grew up in poverty with four other siblings. My father was the only breadwinner, and my mother stayed at home to look after us. Everything was scarce. We had to live on rations and all five of us slept in one small room. For me, being at home, wasn't fun. There was always tension between my parents, and seeing the way we lived was far from inspiring for me. I was looking for any means to not be around that environment, so I was out most of the time, mainly hanging out with guys in the hood who weren't exactly role models for honesty and integrity."

"Wow!" I said surprised. "I would never have guessed that, Josh. Seeing you always relaxed, always cheery, living a happy life, I always imagined you had a loving upbringing."

Joshua chuckled at my comment. "Isn't it interesting, the assumptions we make? We see the end result and assume that it must be due to a loving upbringing or good genes."

"Yes, we do," I said sheepishly. "I admit to sometimes assuming that criminals must have suffered a harsh upbringing."

Joshua continued, "I was obsessed with making money; all I wanted to do was to put an end to this situation my family was in. I couldn't stand seeing my sisters having to settle for old clothes and shoes, feeling embarrassed around their friends who were keeping up with the trends. Having to hear my dad saying we can't afford this, we can't waste that. Seeing my mother trying to feed all seven of us with so little. I'll never forget her face when she knew we were still hungry, but didn't have anything to give us, and I was determined to put an end to it—"

"Gee, Josh!" I interrupted. "That sounds exactly like what I was feeling growing up."

"I know," Joshua smiled. "I did tell you that I could see a lot of you in me."

"So did you put an end to it?" I asked with extended curiosity.

"Luckily, I didn't," Joshua said.

"Luckily!? Why 'luckily'!?" I asked, surprised.

"Because had I done something about it, I wouldn't be here telling the story," he said gravely.

"I don't understand," I said.

Joshua explained, "The gang I was hanging with regularly robbed stores. I never participated in these robberies, but I knew that they were doing it. The day after a robbery, we would gather around the community hall, as we normally did, and they would laugh and brag about it. How much they got, who didn't do what right, and all sorts of details about the robbery. I would be listening and laughing with them, but I never actually had the guts to do it myself. One day, when I felt like I was having a nervous breakdown, I decided enough was enough. I remember the guys talking about how much money the convenience store across the road from the community hall must be making, being open twenty-four hours. They were talking about robbing it and I decided, this time, I was going to have a share in that. We met up at Joey's place and planned the robbery. I was supposed to be the one robbing it if I wanted the bigger share. I was to get 60% and they were going to share the other 40%. It was only going to be a one-off for me. I thought I'd get enough money to come home with lots of food for my mom and clothes for my sisters, and give us a head start.

They gave me a gun and told me where the getaway car was going to be parked. I was supposed to arrive there just before midnight, when it was quiet and the store would be empty of customers, and make a dash in and out and run straight to the getaway car that was parked around the corner. Pretty straightforward.

That night, I was dropped off about half a block from the convenience store, and started walking toward the entrance. I felt apprehensive; something in my gut was churning, but I went ahead anyway. There were no cars outside and no people around, except for a beggar who was lying on the ground near the entrance. I thought nothing of it; he looked like he was asleep with a blanket over his head, and he didn't look like he was capable of stopping a robbery. So, I just ignored him and walked past him. As I walked past, I heard the beggar say, "I wouldn't do it if I were you…Joshua." I froze and turned toward the beggar. "What did you say?" I asked aggressively. The beggar lifted his head up and removed the blanket that was covering his head. His eyes were as blue as the ocean, and his skin was as white as sand. "I said, I wouldn't do it if I were you," he said again with a smile on his face.

"You wouldn't do what!?" I asked with an intimidating voice. "Do you want to die?!" I yelled while I was holding my gun inside my hoodie's pocket, pointing it at the beggar. I kept yelling, "How did you know my name?! How did you know my name!?" I wasn't going to continue until I found out who he was and how he knew my name. This continued for maybe a minute, when suddenly, a police car pulled up at the store, and two officers stepped out. I froze in place, I was certain that the officers were going to notice us, I thought if they searched me, they would find the gun, and it would be game over. To my amazement, they ignored us and walked into the store. I turned away from the beggar, and glanced inside the shop through the window, to try and see what they were doing. My heart was pounding uncontrollably, and my breathing was fast, with sweat dripping down my chin. One officer walked toward the counter, and the other, toward the coffee vending machine. At that point, I realized that this beggar saved my life, that thanks to him stopping me, I avoided a face-off with two officers, who would most definitely have walked into the store right in the middle of the robbery, and I don't need to tell you what that means, do I?"

I nodded in confirmation, staring at Joshua with a look of amazement, eyes wide open, and not being able to speak a word.

"Anyway," Joshua continued, " I only stood there for a few seconds before running for my life. I turned back toward the beggar, but he was gone. Vanished. Dematerialised. Imagine what went through my head at that moment?"

"I know exactly what went through your head, Josh," I said with a soft shaky voice. "The same thing that went through mine when it happened to me three weeks ago."

Joshua continued, "Needless to say, I gave up the robbery that night, but then all I could think of was the beggar. I couldn't get him out of my head. From the time I open my eyes in the morning till I shut them at night, that beggar was on my mind.

This beggar knew what I was about to do, and it seemed he knew in advance what was about to happen, and he came to my rescue. That's the only thing I could make of it at the time. I went home, slipped into bed, shaking and shivering, I covered my head with the blanket, and started sobbing. I realized that I had been seconds away from ending up either dead or in jail for a long time, and that thought was so scary, it gave me an anxiety attack. From that point, I stopped hanging out with the gang. That was the second good thing that happened and the beginning of my awakening.

Two days later, I was walking down to the bus stop, and there he was again, sitting on a park bench near the park. At first, I didn't recognize him, but as I walked passed him, he said, "Sorry for startling you the other night, Joshua, but I had to stop you doing something from which there was no return." Just like you, Sam, I wanted to know how he knew my name. When you told me that you had an interaction with a beggar who said he knew you and knew your name, I realized immediately what was happening to you."

"So that's why you turned pale when I told you, I thought that maybe I offended you. Why didn't you say something?" I asked.

Joshua looked at me, and nodded slightly. "I couldn't interfere with the experience. Had I told you then what it was, it would have put you in a sceptical mindset and may have broken the connection. You had to go into it on your own, Sam." He smiled.

"Was his name Gabe by any chance?" I asked, thinking that maybe we encountered the same beggar.

"He told me his name was Nathaniel. He said he was sent to me by my uncle to help me. My uncle had died five years prior!" Joshua emphasized. "As you can imagine, Sam, this didn't go down well with me. How could my uncle send a beggar to help me? But after what happened at the convenience store, I had no choice but to believe that this beggar was more than met the eye, and he was. After I met with him the second time, I sat there with him on the park bench, and had a conversation that continued into the night. There was this sense of calmness in me that I never felt before. His energy field was so soothing, his deep blue eyes were so mesmerizing, that I was unable to feel any type of aggression or anger. I couldn't stop listening to him. He opened my eyes and showed me that life had a structure, a formula. And that nothing was by chance and by coincidence. We go through life thinking that we have to work everything out; we think we're alone in this journey. We're not aware that we have guides and helpers. Nathaniel was one of them."

I looked at Joshua with gratitude and relief. For three weeks, I'd been trying to make sense of what happened to me, suffering on my own, thinking I was going mad, and of all people, my coworker and close friend, had the exact same experience that would have given me the answers and the proof that I wasn't hallucinating or losing my mind. I was too worried about being ridiculed, or my ego was, to be exact. Maybe this is the first lesson in how damaging and misguiding the ego can be. It actually made me suffer on my own for three weeks unnecessarily.

Joshua continued, "At the end of our encounter, I felt a sense of purpose, a sense of security that I wasn't alone in this journey, and it gave me the strength to trust my purpose and my intended destiny. I understood that each of us has a unique path that contributes to the whole, and that no matter how hard we tried to veer off it, it would catch up with us. Twenty years later, I can see how this is true. In the past twenty years, all the major events in my life happened seemingly out of the blue without me even thinking about them or wishing for them, and some were even the total opposite to what I thought should happen, but they were good, and they were right. I can see it now when I look back at it." Joshua nodded with a proud look on his face. "Ahh, Nathaniel," he murmured. "I called him the guide who saved me."

"Gabe said that he was a beggar by choice. This seems to be a little strange and risky in a sense that they wouldn't be taken seriously, as most of us think of beggars as people who are down on their luck. I know, at first, I had trouble taking Gabe seriously."

Josh smiled while scratching his head. "The reason they choose to come back as beggars is because they need you to listen with your soul and not your ego, and for that to happen, you have to look beyond appearances and judgment. When you don't judge, and you don't assume, you remove the ego from the equation and your heart is open to hearing them, it's open to the truth. They also give you little hints that they're not ordinary beings, like calling you by your name the first time they meet you," Joshua explained. "Those who can't see past that are left alone until they're ready, but they'll keep trying until the end of your time, and they're very patient and persistent."

"They come back? What do you mean, 'they come back'? Who are they? And where do they come back from?" I asked.

"They're guides Sam, they're incarnated souls who choose to come back as guides, rather than souls who reincarnate into a new human experience. Everyone has them Sam; it's just that most don't hear them, particularly when they're too occupied with pleasing the ego. But if you can listen with your soul, they can change your life." He smiled and took a sip of his soda.

"Yeah, it resonated with me. It was almost hypnotic. In a way, just like in your case, he saved my life. I was ready to check myself out. Life was becoming unbearable for me. It was like being inside a dark tunnel, which kept going and going but not a shimmer of light ahead. I remember everything he said, but now I need to put it into practice."

"Sam, there's nothing to put in practice really. Once you start seeing evidence of this truth, you learn to trust the rest and just get on with your life and let it unfold," Joshua said.

"It seems a little strange doesn't it? If my destiny and purpose are already predetermined for me, then why bother hoping and dreaming?" I asked.

Joshua smiled. "When I was living in poverty and saw how hard it was for my family, all I wanted to do was make money. I took upon myself the role of their saviour. My hopes and dreams were about ending this unpleasant situation, which had nothing to do with my path. Ironically, this very situation gave both my sisters the life they have now. They now have a successful business, making affordable designer clothing, marketed specifically for low-income families. By trying to interfere with their destiny, I almost paid the ultimate price. This made me realize, that most hopes and dreams come from a place of dissatisfaction with where we are in life, thinking that achieving these hopes and dreams will give us a more satisfying existence when, in truth, we all have one hope and dream, and that is to be happy. The problem is, we all have different definitions of what being happy means, and we're usually looking for it in the wrong places."

"So I should forget about my dream of opening a restaurant, and having a relationship with Selena?" I asked.

After meeting Nathaniel, I realized that I didn't need hopes and dreams, I just needed patience and trust, and I needed to stop second-guessing how life was meant to unfold. The notion that we all had a unique, predetermined path really did it for me. Thinking that you need to be somewhere or achieve something by a certain time really puts a lot of strain on you, particularly, when what you are trying to achieve isn't part of your destiny. The way Nathaniel put it to me was particularly intriguing. He said, "Joshua, when you came to this world, the movie of your life was already filmed, edited, and published, and you can't change the script. Now, all you have to do is sit and watch it unfold with curiosity as an observer and trust that the parts you don't understand will become clear as the movie progresses. You don't create your life; you reveal it. I repeat that as a mantra every time I feel insecure or anxious."

"Now you sound like Gabe, though Gabe used a different metaphor. He told me to sit in the canoe and enjoy the ride." I laughed.

Joshua joined in my laughter. "Canoe is good too. The point is, Sam, the journey is unique to the individual soul, but the formula is the same for everyone. What Gabe told you is the same as what Nathaniel told me twenty years ago; it's just that I had twenty years to practice it and test it. Now it's your turn, Sam." Joshua raised his bottle and toasted to that.

"Trust me, Sam, when you let go of the burden of trying to figure everything out yourself and stop trying to give everything your own meaning, life becomes a lot more enjoyable; it simply unfolds effortlessly and beautifully as it was designed to, and in perfect timing."

"Can you give me an example?" I asked.

"When I missed the bus to an important job interview, I was angry and bitter. The bus driver saw me running, but he just kept going. I cursed and thought it was the end of the world; I was so disappointed and certain that I missed the job opportunity. Little did I know that the woman who came and sat next to me at the bus stop would become my beautiful wife, my soul mate." He laughed. "Thank God I missed that bus."

"I must admit, Josh, that I was always in awe of how happy you and your family are; there's always warmth and love coming from your house. I was even a little jealous; I wished my family had lived in such harmony."

"Thank you, Sam, and I wouldn't have it any other way. We have everything we need, and we're always conscious about being grateful for what we have. We have a small house, but it's a home. We have food that keeps our bellies full, and we have clothing to keep us warm. But what we don't have is envy or desire for more than we need. The modern-day devil has a new name, it's called *credit,* and its first cousin is called *greed*. People live beyond their means in search of happiness outside of themselves, but they don't realize that this little devil is locking them into a life of slavery to the point where their lives become about paying off debts, with long working hours and high levels of stress, without leaving time for what really matters, like family, love, children, hobbies, and fun. They want more material stuff, big homes, flashy cars, and they borrow more money than they have, so they can feel happy for a day. They end up living to work, and most do work they hate because they put themselves in a position of not having a choice. But they do what they have to do rather than what they love to do in order to pay off the debt they've accrued in the search of happiness. This isn't living; this is a self-imposed prison. It forces them to go down the wrong road to their destination and into a painful correction process."

I looked at Joshua and nodded with agreement. "Gabe did say that we're brainwashed to believe that life is about material possessions, and I can see it now, even in myself. All my insecurities and self-evaluation were based on what I had and didn't have. Living in a derelict apartment, being poor, and working with garbage. I was even making a huge effort to try and hide it from Selena because my ego wouldn't allow me to feel worthy of her, because I don't have much. It made me lie and embarrassed me, and the result was never having the courage to ask her out."

Joshua exploded in a big belly laugh. "Sam, where would people be without us garbage collectors? They would be surrounded by the clutter and stench of their own rubbish. We're an important part that contributes to the whole, we're small nuts in a very big machine, but take those nuts out, and society falls apart. Everyone's job is just as important as the next person's, but Gabe is right, we only notice the ones with the flashy cars and big houses, and we're filled with envy that drives us to self-destruction, wasting our lives trying to be who we're not meant to be. Nobody likes flies, but most don't realize the importance of flies to the eco system, and without them, the garbage we collect and dead matter wouldn't break down. A fly cannot aspire to be a butterfly; its purpose is to be a fly. If you weren't meant to live in a big house or drive a flashy car, but constantly tried to acquire them, then you're a fly who's wasting its life, trying to be a butterfly."

"To be honest with you, Josh, I hope I'm not destined to work with rubbish for the rest of my life. Not that it bothers me now, but I have other ambitions that I would want to accomplish, and I feel that there's more to my journey."

Joshua put his hand on my shoulder, and with a straight face looked me in the eye. "And I promise you, Sam, if those ambitions are part of your destiny, and not ego driven, you will achieve them, and you will achieve them with great ease when the timing is right. Those ambitions are an indication that there's more to your journey. The important thing is to be happy where you are now, no matter what. The interesting thing about staying on your path and not resisting it is that when you accept it, and flow with it, life leads you into where you need to be, but it also leads you out of it, and into where you need to be next. When you resist and decide to take control, because you're not satisfied with where you are now, you interfere with the guiding system, and that's when true suffering happens. You become lost in the woods and go round and round, trying to find your way out."

Chapter 7

Signs and Synchronicities

I told Joshua, "When I saw the beggar on my way here, I was amazed how someone with so little could still find something to smile about and be so grateful and appreciative of the smallest of things. I don't know this man's past and how he got to this point in his life, but he obviously didn't care much about it. He was sitting there smiling and singing with a happy voice, while greeting people who walked past him, regardless of whether they gave him money or not, and passed no judgment. Everyone got a smile and a greeting with a song. People would look at him like he was crazy just because he was singing and moving his body to his songs. Some would walk around him, as if he were a leper, but he would still bless them with a smile. It made me feel ashamed that I used to do it too. For some reason, we think that someone who's happy and singing in the street to themselves, must be mentally ill. This man was actually happier than most people I know.

Such unconditional love really touched me so much that giving him my lunch money was so easy and satisfying."

Joshua grinned and said, "He obviously doesn't care what other people think of him, and, in that sense, he's freer than most people. The need for approval and recognition stops many people from being what they want to be because they worry about what others might think. As you said, you don't know this man's past. Maybe his path led him to where he is now, and he finally found his bliss. Who are we to judge? Your impression was that he had very little in the material sense, but quite possibly, for him, he has enough. He doesn't have a landlord or a mortgage, he doesn't worry about finding money to pay for the new trends, he doesn't worry about bills or car insurance, and maybe he doesn't care much for all these things. One of the biggest mistakes you can make is to look at someone else's path through the point of view of your own path. It will never make sense to you, nor does it have to. It's like reading the synopsis of a different movie to the one you're watching. It'll never make sense and will always be irrelevant,"

"That's right! I agree!" I exclaimed. "It really annoyed me when people looked at me with judgment when I was talking to Gabe. They would give me these 'what are you doing talking to this filthy man' kind of looks. It really annoyed me. He sat there for hours, and not one person gave him money!"

Joshua looked at me with a look of amazement, both eyebrows raised and eyes wide open, as if I had just said the most ridiculous thing ever.

"What!?" I responded with a sharp tone. "Why are you looking at me like that? What did I say?"

"You don't know!?" he asked, surprised,

"Know what?"

Joshua chuckled. "Oh boy!... Sam, they weren't looking at Gabe; they were looking at you!"

"I know!" I said confidently. "They were probably judging me for talking to a homeless beggar."

Joshua burst out in a big belly laugh.

"I don't understand!" I said impatiently. "Why are you laughing?!"

"When I met Nathaniel the second time, I sat on the park bench with him for hours. People started staring at me, giving me weird looks. I thought the same thing as you, that they were being judgmental about me talking to a beggar. Just like you, it irritated me at first. I responded to them aggressively with 'what are you looking at!?' And they would quickly walk away from me. But when they wouldn't stop staring at me, I just ignored them because Nathaniel was so intriguing, and it didn't matter what they were thinking. Then my aunty Silvy walked by. She looked at me and said, 'Damn, Joshua! Who are you talking to!?' I said, 'I'm talking to Nathaniel. Nathaniel, this is my aunty Silvy.' I went on to introduce them, and Oh boy! Did she flip." Joshua let out another big belly laugh. Then, mimicking his aunty's big mamma voice, he continued, "'I knew there was something wrong with you, boy! I knew you needed help!' She went on and on." Joshua kept laughing.

"Why did she say that?" I asked and laughed at the sounds Joshua was making.

"Sam!... Only we could see them!" he exclaimed.

"Excuse me!?"I stopped laughing and my face went straight "What do you mean?!"

"Sam… all those people who were looking at you, were looking at you because they thought you were talking to yourself!" he exclaimed and kept laughing.

I looked at Joshua with a squint in my eyes, looking confused, and trying to make sense of what he was trying to tell me.

"You were seeing Gabe through your mind's eye, but they didn't see him because they weren't attuned to seeing him. Only you saw him. Aunty Silvy basically saw me talking to myself. She saw me sitting there, waving my hands, engaged in a full-blown conversation with myself. Her face went white, if you believe that's possible." He kept laughing. "Just imagine what it looked like from her perspective." Joshua waved his arms, demonstrating what it would look like to her.

I looked at Joshua with a horrified face. Joshua couldn't contain his laughter; he was obviously amused, and enjoying it. At that moment, I had a flashback to the jogger who gave me that look as if I were crazy. The woman pushing the baby carriage, who looked at me when I was throwing a tantrum at Gabe. Now I understood why she walked away from me so quickly. They obviously saw me yelling at a park bench. And all the people who turned their heads in the park where I sat with Gabe by the tree, they all thought I was talking to a tree. And the mother who told her son that I was probably sick when he asked her who I was talking to. I thought they were looking at Gabe, but they were actually looking at me. At that moment, I recalled Gabe saying with a cheeky voice that they were looking at me, and not him. I thought he was being facetious, but he knew that they couldn't see him. *How embarrassing,* I thought to myself. I started to feel a little dizzy, I sat back on the chair with a shocked expression on my face.

"This... just... keeps... getting... better... and weirder..." I said with slow emphasis.

"Don't feel bad, Sam," Joshua comforted me with a chuckle. "I was just as embarrassed and shocked when I realized what was going on. My aunty called my parents that day and recommended that I should go see a shrink for Christ's sake!" He laughed so hard that tears rolled down his cheeks.. "And how do you explain to your parents that you're not crazy, that you were just getting a crash course on life from a guiding angel?"

Joshua was obviously quite amused at this revelation to me. He couldn't stop laughing and kept poking fun at me. "I'm glad you're amused," I replied in defense. "Are there other weird parts I should know about while we're at it?" I asked with sarcasm in my voice.

"Well, Sam, as weird as it may seem, the way we see our lives is far weirder, don't you think? But now, thanks to what you call weird, I wake up every morning with no expectations for my day. Whatever happens that day will be a surprise, and I welcome it with an open heart because I know that this is exactly what was meant to happen that day. As you know, if you don't expect, you don't get disappointed," he said with a cheeky tone. " We were lucky enough to be able to hear Gabe and Nathaniel. But so many people are so busy trying to control and shape their lives the way they think they should be, that they never hear their guides. Despite the fact that we all have them, not all of us are attuned to hearing them or even know that we have them. There's so much noise in our heads; there's always so much to do, and when we take a break from doing, we watch the boob tube or surf the Web. It creates so much clutter that we can't hear anything. When was the last time you gave your brain a break from thinking? When was the last time you put your mind on silent mode? It's like standing close to a freeway, and trying to hear the birds singing."

I nodded at Joshua with agreement. "Yeah, I definitely could use a break from thinking, and the thing is, the more I think, the worst the scenarios get."

"Sam, we're divine beings," he said with smiling eyes. "We're not some random accident of protoplasm coming together, or a by-product of some big bang. The system we were made to trust and became familiar with wants you to believe that you're insignificant, that you have no purpose and no value. We're not created out of chaos, and we can't thrive in chaos. We're a fragment of a very intelligent system, and each of us is as significant as the sun and the moon and the stars. We're all special, made with love to receive love. Never forget that, Sam. "

"I hear you, Josh," I said softly. "I know exactly what you're saying. Gabe called it brainwashing."

Joshua laughed. "And I call it social standardizing, sort of a 'one size fits all.' We become easier to manage and control that way. We're nothing special according to the mainstream."

I laughed and nodded with agreement. "And speaking of 'special,'" I said with a cheery voice, "I think I should tell Selena how I feel about her, don't you think?"

"I think it's a good idea, Sam!" Joshua confirmed enthusiastically. "I'm sure she would be honored by the gesture."

"I hope so," I said tentatively. "I feel a lot more confident in myself thanks to Gabe and you. If she rejects my gesture, then, at least, I'll know and stop obsessing about it in my head. It's sort of killing me."

Joshua smiled a big smile, and nodded in agreement. "Anything that we hold in is killing us. Remember , Sam, whatever happens is what needs to happen with no judgment or overanalysis. If Selena is meant to be a part of your journey, she will be," he said compassionately. "Life is a game; it's not to be taken seriously. Nothing is permanent and nothing is fixed. It's a journey and the goal isn't to get there; the goal is to enjoy the scenery while you're on your way there. This is one of the most profound things Nathaniel told me, and I kept this in mind my whole life."

"I hear you, Josh," I said, smiling. "I'm getting much better at understanding this; I even stopped buying lottery tickets."

"Well, Sam, there's nothing wrong with buying lottery tickets, provided it's just for fun, and not as a must have to solve your problems. If you win, though, don't forget your friends." Joshua laughed.

I laughed and gave Joshua a hug. "Josh, how could I ever forget you; you're my only friend and I'm grateful for you being in my life."

132

"Likewise, Sam," Joshua replied, looking at me with his sparkling smiling eyes.

The shed door's opened and Louisa came in. "How's the fraternity going?" she asked cheerfully.

"Oh, it's going very well, sweetheart. In fact, it's going so well that Sam's even going to tell his love interest how he feels about her," Joshua joked and winked at me.

"Love interest!" Louisa exclaimed. "She must be a very special girl." She laughed.

Louisa was always keen to know why I didn't have a girlfriend. She used to always ask me how come no one snatched me up by now, but I quickly stepped in to correct the assumption. "Not so fast! I don't even know if she likes me like that; let's not be hasty with the compliments."

"Well, Sam, for what it's worth, I think you'd make a woman very happy one day, and whoever she is will be very lucky. So who is this love interest?" Louisa kept digging.

"Just a waitress at Frank's Diner," I replied with a shy voice. "But I don't think she knows that I like her. I was always very timid around her, but now I feel a bit more confident telling her."

Louisa smiled as she noticed the blush on my face, "Sam, each of us has a soul mate waiting to cross paths with us, and I have no doubt that yours is just as eager to meet you, and there's no telling when or where." She said in her sweet motherly tone, then pointed at Joshua with her eyes. "I met this man at a bus stop, and, believe me, he didn't

133

look too appealing at first. He was angry and frustrated when I met him because he had missed the bus. I remember thinking, *Good Lord, if this is how he reacts to missing a bus, thank God he didn't miss a plane,*" she joked. "But the next bus took long enough to arrive, and it gave us enough time to connect and realize that we had a special bond, and twenty years later, I can tell you that I won the jackpot." She laughed and hugged Joshua.

Joshua kissed her on the head, then looked at me and winked. "I told you, Sam, I give thanks to that bus driver who didn't wait for me every day. Although he looked like a jerk to me at the time, I now know he was a godsend, and look what he sent me." He laughed and squeezed Louisa close to him. "No guarantee I would be as grateful to the pilot if he left without me, though," he joked.

"I'm happy for both of you," I said, smiling. "And I'm pretty sure that when I'm ready, it'll happen for me also. No need to rush; all in good time."

Joshua cheered a loud "yippy" at me. "Now you're talking! You're already grasping the concept," he enthused.

I looked at both of them with grateful, soft, smiling eyes, feeling a sense of belonging, knowing that I had this family in my life. "Well, I better get going," I said with a soft voice. "I've taken enough of your time, Josh, and I appreciate you shedding this light on me. I don't know what I would do without your input."

"You're most welcome, Sam! I'm glad that you've decided to open up to me." He grabbed my hand, pulled me toward him, and gave me a big fatherly hug.

134

"Thank you for the sandwiches Mrs. Jacks... Louisa," I said, quickly correcting myself. Louisa laughed and gave me a hug and a kiss on the cheek. "Take care, Sam," she said lovingly. "You're always welcome here."

"Thank you; that's very kind," I said and walked out of the shed and out through the back gate, waving goodbye to them. They stood there hugged, waving back at me. It reminded me of the good old days, when my parents used to see me off when I was on my way to school. They would stand there on the porch and wish me a good day. When I closed the gate behind me, I would look back at them and see them wave goodbye, standing there hugging like a happy couple. I would wave back and smile. At that time, if you told me that in two years, my mother would be leaving and my father will be crippled, I'd tell you that you were crazy.

I wonder where that beggar is, I thought when I walked past where he had been sitting earlier. I wondered, Did he make enough money to get by today? Where would he be sleeping tonight? Is he really happy and content?. My mind was dwelling on many things. Today had been an emotional rollercoaster. The time at the library, butterflies and spirits, the talk with Joshua, and everything else that happened left me a little too overwhelmed. Everything felt so surreal as if I had just crossed through a portal to another world. As I walked through the park on my way home, I could smell the blossoms, something I hadn't noticed until now. The birds were flying happily from tree to tree, and the setting sun was casting its golden rays on the scattered cirrus clouds, that took the shape of dancing angels. I stood there admiring this picturesque setting, looking at the birds flying unrestricted and singing happily with the golden angels in the sky. A sense of calmness was taking over me as I watched this picture-perfect scene. It was the same feeling I had when I sat here with Gabe, and I thought for a minute that maybe he was near. I looked around, hoping to see him somewhere near, but he wasn't. I took a deep breath, as if I were taking this majestic energy deep into my psyche, and exhaled slowly. Maybe Josh was right; maybe Gabe did what he intended to do and now was helping someone else. I wondered how the next person would react to meeting Gabe. This thought made me smile and giggle at the same time. Or maybe Gabe was assigned to me only; this was also a possibility. I just wished I could thank him one last time. Thank him for saving my life. Maybe I'll never see Gabe again, but the spirit he left in me, means he'll be with me all the time. This was comforting to me. I didn't feel alone and helpless anymore; he left a feeling of assurance in me that made me feel strong. It made me feel as though I could grab life by the horns and look forward to whatever challenge it would throw at me.

It was a nice feeling that I hadn't experienced in a long time. The last time I felt it was when I was a little boy, when I felt safe and secure with my parents around. After they were gone, I was always worried and anxious about the future, and I forgot what it was like to feel safe again, to feel shielded from harm. So, to be able to have this feeling again was just wonderful. I took a deep breath, exhaled slowly, and said, "Thank you, Gabe." I looked up at the dancing angels; they were fading away as the sun disappeared below the horizon. "Thank you, angels. Please say hello to Gabe for me," I said with a soft whisper. As I stood there, looking at the cirrus clouds dissipating, the red and black butterfly landed on my shoulder again.

"Hello again!" I said with a broken emotional voice. I put my finger in front of it, suggesting that it would jump on my finger, and it did. I was amazed. I started to feel my heart pounding faster.

"This is the same butterfly that came to me at the library today!" I whispered to myself. I moved my hand inches from my face and looked closely at the butterfly. The butterfly looked at me right in the eye. His eyes were moving back and forth rapidly. It was as if he were analyzing me, as if he were communicating with me. I looked back into his eyes and said softly, "Is that you, Gabe?!" The butterfly flapped its wings rapidly, and flew away.

I stood there watching the butterfly disappear into the distance, a tear rolled down my cheek. I felt an overwhelming rush through my body. Maybe I did cross through a portal into another world. Gabe said we were living in a holographic reality, so maybe I crossed over to the real world. If a hologram is seen with the mind, maybe my mind doesn't see it anymore? I mean, I talk to butterflies, I met a Beggar, who's the disembodied spirit of a CEO who committed suicide thirty years ago, and angels danced in the sky. I mean, you don't see these kinds of things every day, and maybe this is what it's like living outside of the hologram? I pondered it for a second; it was a thought I felt I should carry with me forever. I felt as if I were waking up from a deep coma. That idea somewhat appealed to me and made me feel good, so why not stay there?

It was getting late, and the next appealing thought that came to me was that I better get home. It was getting cold and dark; I was tired and exhausted and truly ready to call it a day. On my way home, I stopped at Remi's to pick up a few ingredients. I picked a couple of things off the shelf, and walked to the front counter. Remi was serving a female customer; they were laughing and giggling to each other. They were obviously into each other, and I didn't want to break up the moment, so I stood behind her and waited for them to finish while pulling faces at Remi, suggested that he was a flirt. She paid Remi, still giggling. Remi, with his eyes still lit up, said, "Have a good night, Selena," as she went out the door and waved to her.

"Selena!?" I said with a loud surprised voice. "Is her name Selena?!"

"Calm down, boy!" Remi retorted. "What's the big deal? She can have any name she wants, as long as she keeps coming here," he said with a jolly Jamaican accent and chuckled. "Why are you so surprised?" Remi asked suspiciously. "Does the name Selena mean something to you? A secret love maybe?" he kept teasing.

I stood there looking at Remi with a stunned face. Here I was, at the end of an emotional day, filled with signs and magical synchronicities, getting another obvious communication from my soul, Remi had a crush on a woman called Selena, and I just happened to be there to witness it.

"Well, as a matter of fact, it does mean something to me," I said with a cheeky smirk on my face. "Probably as much as it does to you, by the looks of it." I laughed and gave him the money for the groceries.

Remi laughed and handed me the change. "I'm scared to ask her out," he admitted.

"Oh, I know exactly how you feel," I said sympathetically. "I've known my Selena for months now, and I still can't bring myself to ask her out."

"Yeah! What is with us, maan?!" he replied. "Why do we get all shy and scared when we like someone?"

I looked at Remi in the eye and started grinning. "A wise man I met recently told me it's because our egos don't cope well with rejections, and a rejection from someone we like is its biggest fear."

"I think that wise maan is right, Sammy Boy. I don't think I'd be able to bear her rejection, so, at least, I live in a fantasy world with her in it. Better than nothing, right!?" He laughed.

I laughed and nodded in sympathy. No one could understand Remi's situation better than I could. "See you, Remi! Good luck!" I said cheerfully and walked out.

Wow! I thought to myself. *What are the odds of that happening at this time?* It gave me a glimpse into what Gabe was talking about. I mean, Selena isn't exactly a common name. Was that a sign that I should talk to Selena? I know, for a fact, that if I hadn't met Gabe, I probably would have treated this scenario as a coincidence, but this was what he talked about when he explained that the universe speaks to us and gives us direction through signs and synchronicities. I think I was just given a firsthand demonstration of that. It made me feel confident, and, at that point, I felt fully charged and enthusiastic, the feeling of fear was dissipating and a feeling of courage emerged. I walked home, feeling light in my chest and elated.

"I can do it! I can do it!" I chanted enthusiastically and stepped into my apartment building. This time, I wasn't looking at the state of the building. I wasn't snarling at the run down foyer, or scoffing at the stench in the stairwell, as I normally did. It was almost as if I were happy to be there. This was a pleasant change because paying attention to those details only made me feel worse about my situation, and now, it looked as though I finally learned to accept my situation.

When I entered my apartment, I didn't even care that the answering machine showed zero messages. I used to see it as a reminder of my loneliness, but not this time. This time, I just saw it as a number on a square box and gave it no meaning. This was another noticeable change in me. *Wow! This is very cool!* I thought to myself. *I can get used to this way of living.* I laughed and dropped myself on the bed, springing up and down a couple of times, and just lay there.

I was waiting to fall asleep. My mind was racing over the events of the day, but in the end, I settled on just one thought, Selena. How would I approach her? What would I say? And all sorts of different scenarios, but in my mind, the outcome was the same; she'd say yes, and we'd be together. I felt so confident, and, in my mind, I could see us walking happily along the river, hugging and laughing and even kissing. My eyes started to become heavy, and, with a grin on my face, I slowly shut my eyes and whispered, "Goodnight, Selena."

Chapter 8

Selena Lost and Found

I woke up the next morning to the sound of a domestic argument and plates being smashed on the wall by Mick and Donna, the couple next door. Their domestic fights are a common occurrence, and, normally, I'd grunt and be disturbed by them, but, this time, I lay in bed, staring at the ceiling with a smirk on my face. Another plate hit the wall and smashed against it. It jolted me, but despite that, the grin on my face was getting bigger. Though I would hate to associate Selena with this commotion, she was the first thing on my mind when I opened my eyes, and it was pleasant enough to override the unpleasantness of Mick's expression of dissatisfaction with his breakfast.

I never understood why people feel the need to express themselves so violently. Why are Mick and Donna still together? This couple haven't had a day without arguing and fighting; they must have used up most of their crockery by now. Yet they still find it imperative to share a small space together. Maybe this is what happens when you're stuck in a rut when you resist the changes that the Universe is telling you to make and become accustomed to the status quo. The fear of being alone causes you to hold onto someone you don't get along with. The pressure on you grows, as you continue to resist moving on and the accumulated resentment creates irrational behavior. I can't imagine treating someone you love like that, but who am I to judge, right?

Maybe this is why my mother left? The idea that if you're unhappy where you are means that you're not where you're supposed to be came to mind. Maybe it will help me understand and accept that my mother was simply unhappy where she was and simply moved on toward happiness. It still didn't give me the answer to why she wouldn't at least keep in touch with me, and I always hoped that one day, I'd get to ask her that. But I don't even know where she is, or if she's alive. Since meeting Gabe, I learned to give the benefit of a doubt and not judge or assume, so I'll avoid doing that even in my mother's case, and as hard as it may be, I want to believe that there was a reason that I can't see right now.

Things finally settled down next door. I guess Mick got his bacon crispy enough. I got out of bed with a spring in my step and got ready for my special day, when I would finally open up to Selena. I felt good about it. I was humming and whistling as I was getting ready. I poured myself a cup of coffee from the percolator, and stood there in the kitchen, rehearsing different ways to approach her about it.

I took the last sip of my coffee, put the cup in the sink, straightened my jacket, exhaled sharply as if I were about to enter an examination that would decide whether I'd live or die, and walked out of the apartment.

142

It was a fine crisp morning, and I didn't know if the tremors I felt were due to the coolness of the morning, or my nervous system kicking into overdrive. I was so confident prior to this moment, but as I got closer to Frank's Diner, I started to feel more and more apprehensive. Suddenly, I heard a voice in my head, saying, "What if she says no? What if I become speechless? What if everybody laughs at me?" Yesterday and this morning, I felt unstoppable; I received a clear sign that I should do it, and it empowered me, but now, all of a sudden, as I approach Frank's Diner, I felt fear and resistance, as if I were about to step into an execution room. Was this feeling coming from my ego's fear of rejection? Or was it coming from my intuition telling me not to do it? Gabe's words suddenly started playing in my head. The words that said that our intuition makes us feel good about something we're supposed to do, and it will always overcome the resistance, and with that in mind, I found myself right in front of Frank's front door. I didn't even realize that I was walking toward the front door. "The intuition won again," I said to myself, laughing, and proceeded to enter the diner. The cowbell on the door chimed as I opened it, I stuck my head in first and looked around inside. There were a few people having breakfast and reading the paper. I looked around trying to spot Selena. Suzie the waitress was running around serving coffees, then she spotted me.

"Hey, Sam! Long time no see!" she greeted me.

"Hi Suzie!" I greeted her back and kept scouring the place with my gaze, trying to spot Selena, but I couldn't see her anywhere.

"Take a seat; I'll be with you in a minute," she said cheerfully and continued her coffee top up run.

My usual booth near the door was taken, so I took the one at the very end. It also gave me a bit of privacy to be far from other diners, that way, no one will hear me when I start my intimate conversation with Selena. I sat in the booth, and kept looking around for Selena, but I still couldn't see her. I was getting a little worried, because she was always here on Thursdays. *Maybe she stepped out for a minute, or was having a break*, I thought to myself.

Suzie approached my booth with a big smile on her face.

"How are you, sweetheart?" she said cheerfully. "Where've you been all this time?" she asked with her vivacious voice.

"I've been soul searching," I joked.

"Haven't we all?" she replied with a chuckle. "Shame," she said and sat down in the opposite side of the booth.

"Shame because I've been soul searching? Or shame I haven't been here?" I replied cheerfully.

"Well, shame you haven't been here because Selena would have loved to say goodbye to you," she said.

At that moment, I felt like my world just caved in on me. Not only was Selena gone, but the confusion and disappointment about why my intuition and my soul would give me a sign and lead me toward something that would prove fruitless, was painful. I felt cheated. I felt angry inside.

"When did she leave? Where did she go?" I asked with a shaky voice.

144

"She left two weeks ago. She didn't get her scholarship and had to leave the university. She decided to go traveling and clear her head, but she didn't say where she was going," Suzie explained. "She was constantly wishing that you'd come in so she'd get a chance to say goodbye to you. She even considered looking for you at work." Suzie exhaled a long sigh. "I miss her," she said with a tone of longing.

"Wait a minute!" I said, surprised. "What do you mean she considered looking for me at work? Does she know where I work?" I asked with a tremor in my voice and a look of horror on my face.

"She knew you worked at the Garbage Depot, but she didn't want to embarrass you unless you told her yourself," Suzie explained. "I'd give you her cell number, but, apparently, it's been disconnected; she must be in a different state."

I felt my heart sinking deeper into my chest. I just realized that all this time, Selena knew the things I was too embarrassed to tell her. I realized that while I was trying to hide it from her and lying about my situation, she actually knew the truth. They all knew the truth! This made me feel like a complete loser. The pressure in my chest was getting more intense, and my breathing was getting shallower. I felt as if cold sweat was covering my face. Suzie noticed me being upset, she took my hand, looked me in the eye, and with a soft compassionate tone said, "It's okay, Sam; she didn't care where you worked. Selena would never care about things like that. She liked you regardless; she thought you were a really nice guy." She giggled.

I know that Suzie was trying to make me feel better; she obviously thought that I was upset because of the embarrassment of being caught lying about my job. That was partially true, but she obviously didn't know about my real feelings for Selena, and what she really

145

meant to me, so how could she understand the true impact of this news?

Suzie looked at me with her smiling eyes. "I have to go back to work, Sam," she said apologetically. "Do you want me to order your milkshake in the meantime?" she asked.

My head was still lowered. I paused for a second then lifted my head up slowly.

"Thanks, Suzie, but I don't feel like one today," I said sadly with a fake smile and got up. "I better get going. Thank you, Suzie," I said and rushed to the front door.

Suzie looked at me surprised. "Oh, okay! Are you okay, Sam?"

I smiled forcefully. "Yeah, everything's fine; I just remembered I need to be somewhere," I said in an attempt to defuse the situation and walked out of the diner. This time, I didn't look back; there was no point because Selena wasn't there to look back at. I would no longer enjoy her smile, her lisp, and how she sounded when she said my name, the happy voice, and the dangling ponytail. I thought of all the things I wouldn't be seeing anymore. I felt very disappointed and sad, and all the elation and confidence that I had felt the day before just dissipated. I felt angry and betrayed by my soul. I resented it for being so cruel to me, for dangling a carrot in front of me, only to retract it quickly, as soon as I reached out to it.

"Don't give it a meaning, Sam! If it's not in your favor, it ain't over yet!" a voice sounded in my head, but it was very loud, it was like God used some kind of a megaphone from up above and yelled it

146

down to me. I stood there and looked around to see where the voice was coming from.

"What?! Is that you Gabe?!" I asked loudly.

The look on the faces of passersby was all too familiar to me. Here I was again, talking to an invisible entity in the middle of the street. But the voice was more than just a passing thought; it sounded so real, like it came from outside of me. I shook my head in disappointment, looked up, and sarcastically said, "Thanks for nothing!"

"If it's not in your favor, it ain't over yet," I mumbled scornfully. "What do you mean it ain't over yet?!" I stood there and yelled at the sky in anger, "It is over! and it's not in my favor!" my voice was getting louder, and angrier. "Selena is gone!" I yelled with a broken voice. "My soul gave me a sign that I should speak to her, and I followed through, but what my soul didn't know was that she left two weeks ago. Some perfect timing!" I muttered with sarcasm. I shook my head in disappointment and walked home.

That evening I lay on the bed, staring at the ceiling, literally frozen in place. Many thoughts were running through my head, trying to make sense of everything. *Maybe it doesn't work for me? Maybe all that stuff that Gabe and Joshua were talking about doesn't apply to me? Maybe all the stuff that Gabe told me about sitting in the canoe and letting life carry you, doesn't work on me?* The thoughts kept running in all directions *Maybe my soul isn't calibrated and missed the right timing? Maybe I'm jinxed? Maybe Remi talking to a woman by the name Selena was merely a coincidence?* I tried every approach and any possibility.

I felt alone again. I felt that my inner friend who gave me the hope and feeling of security had abandoned me and, now, I was left to fend for myself. I felt scared. I grabbed the pillow and pressed it close to my chest and shut my eyes.

I must have exhausted myself with all the thinking and analyzing because I slept so deeply that I missed the alarm and was awakened by the phone ringing. I jumped out of bed in panic after realizing that I'd slept through the alarm and picked up the phone.

"Hello..." I answered with a tired voice.

Joshua was on the other line. "Good afternoon!" he greeted me sarcastically, suggesting it was late in the day.

"Sorry, Josh, I'll be there in fifteen minutes," I quickly answered.

Josh laughed. "See you soon!" he said and hung up.

Like a raving lunatic, I rushed to get dressed. I knew how much Joshua hated to start late, and, to be honest, I hated it too. The later we started, the longer the shift became because the increase in traffic and pedestrians slowed us down.

Lucky, I'm a fast runner, I arrived at the depot in record time. Joshua stood there, tapping his watch impatiently at me. I ran straight to him and with what remained of my breath, apologized profusely.

"That's alright, Sam," he said cheerfully. "I hope it's due to a worthy cause." He laughed and tapped the side of the truck to get it going. I jumped on the back step of the truck, still huffing and puffing from the sprint to the depot, and almost lost my grip. Joshua laughed loudly, amused and entertained by my near slip, but I wasn't in a position to object to anything after being late and possibly extending Joshua's day; I just let him enjoy himself.

"At least you got the heart kick-started," Joshua poked fun at me. "Straight into second gear, because that's where we need to switch to, young man." He laughed and raised his eyebrows quickly in an attempt to tease me.

I smiled, nodded in agreement, and looked ahead in the direction the truck was going, anticipating the first stop.

"Wow! No comeback?!" Joshua teased me. "Are you alright?!" he kept teasing, but I just stood there quietly, not retaliating, looking ahead. "Usually you'd have something to say back, you're not maturing on me now, are you?" Joshua kept poking at me, trying to get a rise out of me.

I turned my head to Joshua and with a straight face said, "I don't think this stuff is working for me."

Joshua looked at me with a confused look. "What stuff?" he asked.

"That 'soul' stuff that Gabe was talking to me about," I yelled over the truck's revving engine.

"How so?" Joshua yelled back as the noise from the hydraulic pump gotten louder.

"Remember when I told you that I should tell Selena how I feel about her?" Joshua nodded in confirmation. "Well, after leaving your house, I received a pretty clear confirmation that I should do it, just like Gabe and Nathaniel said happens, and I followed through."

149

"Great! How did it go?" Joshua asked.

"Not too good, and this is the point. She left two weeks ago," I said.

"So you're wondering why you got a sign that supposedly lead you to a disappointment," Joshua said with a chuckle.

"Yeah! Basically!" I replied. "The nature of it, and the timing of it, was quite clear."

"Clear to whom?" Joshua asked abruptly. "You made your own interpretation of it, and you decided that that was what the sign meant, and you built up your expectations based on your interpretations, and now you're heart broken and disappointed that the outcome you thought it would lead to didn't happen. Am I close?"

I nodded in agreement. "Yes, you are, but you can't blame me for making such interpretations. After all, it was a perfect timing. What else could I have made it out to be?"

"You made it out to be exactly what it is, an instruction to go and see Selena. It's your expectations of a certain outcome that created this turmoil in you. Maybe you were supposed to find out that Selena is gone for some reason, particularly at such time. I can't tell you why because I don't know, and I don't want to assume, but maybe the name Selena has a significant meaning to you, and maybe that's what the sign was trying to emphasize. What it means exactly, I can't tell you, but what I can tell you is that nothing is random and everything is intelligently intertwined. I guess you'd just have to let the rest reveal itself in its due time," Joshua said with a smile.

"Yeah, the name Selena is definitely significant to me, but now for the wrong reasons. It's a reminder of a loss, rather than gain," I said in a bitter disappointed tone.

"It's not over yet, Sam. There's still a lot you're not seeing right now. Don't try to build the full picture with only a few pieces. The remaining pieces don't rest with you; be patient."

I looked at Joshua with a look of admiration. "I'm pretty sure that you're an important part of my destiny, Josh. You make it sounds so logical." I chuckled and continued emptying bins into the back of the truck.

"I clocked up years of practice and plenty of evidence to support it," he said. "I was too overly scrutinizing when I first learned how it worked. I was testing it, and, more often than not, I was trying to guess what everything meant, and each time I thought I knew what it meant, I received a completely different outcome. I finally stopped trying to guess, and conceded that the language I was spoken to, was a language I am yet to understand. Not only was I very bad at it but it also made me step out of the flow, holding on so tight to ideas. It made me rigid and was too much hard work. When I didn't care so much about what everything meant, I finally understood how it works. I finally started to understand the Universal Language."

I looked at Joshua with a conniving grin on my face. "Then I guess there's a very good reason why I slept through the alarm today," I joked.

Joshua laughed. "Possibly, but whatever it is, it better be good because we're way behind schedule and the traffic is getting busier."

"I hear you!" I said with a tone of compliance and tapped the side of the truck, signalling the driver to move forward.

The truck started moving, trying to get out of this narrow lane, and into the main street. Both Josh and I were standing on the back step, trying to avoid being hit by the walls of the narrow lane, when the truck suddenly stopped.

"What's going on?" I asked.

Joshua peered over the side of the truck. "Damn! Pedestrians crossing," he replied impatiently. "We're gonna be here forever," he sighed.

"A minute ago you were talking about being patient, so back at you!" I teased Joshua.

Joshua laughed. "Nicely played, Sam! Thanks for the reminder. I need them sometimes."

Suddenly, we heard a blood-curling scream coming from the main street. It sounded like a woman was in serious trouble. Both Joshua and I jumped off the truck, and ran toward where the screams were coming from. A woman was lying on the ground yelling, "My bag! He stole my bag; please help!" The thief obviously tried to snatch the bag off the woman's hand but she didn't let go and he dragged her a few yards before she finally let go. Her right knee was grazed and bloody and her suit was covered in dirt. Joshua picked the woman up of the ground. I could see the thief running in the distance, and, without hesitation, I started running after him.

I was slowly gaining on the thief, I kept my eyes on him as he was trying to cut through side lanes and buildings. He was jumping fences and running through busy streets, but I kept gaining on him, closer and closer. He finally realized that I had a good chance of catching him, and let go of the bag. I picked up the bag and quickly ran back to the woman.

She was sitting on the bench, trying to clean the dirt off her jacket, when she spotted me running toward her. She got up quickly, and once she realized I was holding her bag, her face lit up and a huge smile emerged on her face. I thought, *wow, what a beautiful smile.*

"Here you go," I said, handing the bag to her while trying to catch my breath.

"My knight in shining armor! Thank you so much!" she said emotionally, and went to give me a hug.

"I wouldn't do that if I were you," I said while still catching my breath, and stopped her from getting closer. She took a step back.

"Sorry, I didn't mean to offend you; it's just that I'm currently wearing a selection of Detroit's garbage," I said sheepishly.

"Well I'm not much better," she said, pointing to her dirty skirt and jacket. She handed me my gloves, which I had dropped when I ran after the thief. "Here, these are yours I believe," she said, smiling.

"Well, I guess I'm your knight in dirty gloves," I said, laughing and thanked her for the gloves. "I have to go back to work," I said reluctantly. She was so beautiful and lovely. Her smile was mesmerizing. I definitely would have loved to have given her more of my time, and the truth is, I didn't want to leave, but I had to rush back to the truck. I caused enough delay by being late, and the last thing I wanted was to delay Joshua even more.

"I have to thank you for this courageous act," she said. "You've saved my life, which, sadly enough, is entirely in this bag. How about dinner at my house on Sunday? Please, I insist!" she said stubbornly.

"I don't know; are you sure?!" I asked, surprised, and pulled on my shirt, suggesting I'm working in garbage.

"I'm absolutely sure," she said enthusiastically and extended her hand toward me. "I'm Selena," she said and shook my hand.

Oh boy! I thought to myself. My eyes opened wide in shock. Suddenly, I felt a shiver going up and down my spine, and my jaw became agape. I shook her hand slowly and gently with a shocked look on my face. My stare was frozen, looking into her eyes, and, with a stutter, I said, "I... I'm S...Sam... S...Sam King."

"Nice to meet you, Sam King," she said cheerfully. "Are you okay? You look like you've just seen a ghost." She laughed.

"Oh... I... I'm fine," I reassured her quickly. "Just trying to catch my breath."

"Okay then," she said with a smile, handing me a piece of paper. "Here's my address and cell number. How does 6 p.m. sound?" she asked.

"S...six is fine!" I said while still trying to process the strange coincidence. No wonder she noticed my reaction. I stood there like a

154

teenager who was confronted by their rock idol, speechless and with a look of shocked admiration on my face. I definitely didn't have time to explain why her name made me react like that. I took the note and said, "Thank you, Selena; I'll see you then."

"No, thank you! My knight in dirty gloves," she said, giggling.

Joshua and the truck were farther down the road, continuing the run without me, while Joshua was doing twice the work, covering for me. I ran as fast as I could, trying to catch them. *This must be one of those days where running is the theme of the day,* I thought to myself. *Since opening my eyes this morning, all I'm doing is running. Running to work, running after thieves, and now here I am, in the middle of another sprint to the truck.* I thought my heart was going to explode.

I finally caught up with the truck. Joshua was tipping bins at twice the rate and looking tired.

"Sorry, Josh! But you ain't gonna believe this!" I said while trying to catch my breath and almost fainting.

"I ain't gonna believe getting home for supper," he replied cheekily.

I quickly took back my side and relieved Joshua of having to do the bins on both sides. I could see on his face that he wasn't too impressed, so I picked up the pace in an attempt to redeem myself.

"Her name is Selena," I randomly yelled out to Joshua.

Joshua looked at me with confusion. "Who's name is Selena?" he yelled over the truck's roaring engine.

"That woman I just saved. Her name is Selena." I smiled and kept tipping bins into the back.

Joshua looked at me intensely, and a smile started growing on his face. "Well, well, I bet you didn't see that coming," he said, laughing.

"No, I didn't. It wasn't on my list of possibilities, I must admit," I joked.

"And that's why we should leave the guess work out of the equation," Joshua said with slight sarcasm. He seemed almost as excited as I was by what was happening to me.

"And she invited me over for dinner on Sunday night," I said with a smirk on my face, waiting to see Josh's reaction.

"Holy smokes!" he retorted. "Now, I don't want to jump to conclusions, but it's quiet clear to me what's going on. Can you see that, Sam?" he asked.

I pulled the note she gave me and placed it open in front of Josh's face. "And look where she lives," I teased.

"And a rich one too!" Josh exclaimed. "It looks like the Universe did have a different plan for you after all," he said.

"And... she already knows where I work, so no burden in telling her." I wiggled with excitement and crashed two bin lids together like a big band crescendo.

"Okay, calm down!" Joshua signalled. "You still have to get passed her parents," he said, laughing.

"Her parents?!" I said, surprised. "What makes you think she lives with her parents?"

Joshua said, "You don't think she lives at that address on her own, do you?"

Joshua had a point. The address was in a very rich neighbourhood, and Selena looked too young to have accumulated that kind of wealth.

"If that's the case, then I'm sure they'll know about me before I arrive," I said with a cheeky grin on my face. "Besides, her name is Selena, and it has to mean something, right?"

Joshua smiled. "After the lessons of the past few days, I sure wouldn't jump to any conclusions or make any assumptions, but yeah, Selena seems to appear prominent lately."

"Hmmm..." I mumbled and stood there with a thoughtful look on my face. "Maybe being late was part of the plan after all," I said. "Had we started at our normal time, I wouldn't have been at the crime scene."

"It's very possible, Sam, but those things become clear in hindsight. We don't know the reason behind every single piece, until they reveal their purpose in the puzzle. Right now, just enjoy yourself and don't worry about whether it has a major purpose for your life or not; just have fun and embrace whatever outcome with no expectations. No expectations, no disappointments." Joshua pulled a cheesy smile and winked. He then clapped his hands to hurry us along. "Come on! Let's finish this run already," he commanded.

We were nearing the end of the run, and in spite of everything that happened, we were only about two hours behind schedule. That meant Joshua would get home before supper. I, on the other hand, was completely lost in thoughts, and for the rest of the run, I was in dreamland. Joshua was laughing because he knew what was going on in my head, and I think that the ballet steps I was making prior to tipping a bin also gave it away.

It felt like the Universe took one Selena and replaced her with another. I was so astounded. It truly did feel as though we are playing Treasure Trove with the Universe, and I was starting to see it even more. Considering I started the day with doubt and negativity toward this concept and Gabe's teachings, this was a blessing.

I now know what Gabe meant when he said that we're too busy or ignorant to be able to notice the signs. When I look back at my short life, I can see a lot of similar occurrences that happened to me, but I either didn't know what they meant or I simply dismissed them as either good luck, bad luck, or coincidence. I was giving them a meaning, and this is exactly what Gabe warned me against. Now that I'm aware that we have a guidance system, I'm a lot more receptive to them and notice them a lot more.

We finally got to the end of the run. We picked up the last bin and headed back to the depot. I was standing on the back step of the truck, swaying like I was on a merry-go-round, as the truck increased its speed.

"Settle down, Tiger," Joshua joked with a smirk on his face. "You don't want to end up having your dinner in a hospital ward, do you?"

I looked at Joshua with a big grin on my face, and batted my eyelids in an attempt to tease him.

Josh rolled his eyes, shook his head, and muttered, "The boy is in love."

I wasn't sure if *in love* was the correct term, but I was definitely over the moon and excited about this new turn of events. I think it would be a while before everything truly sank in, but for now, I was just happy to have some form of excitement in my life. This "something to look forward to" feeling I hadn't experienced since I was six years old, when my father told me a week before Christmas, that he had received a call from Santa, saying he was going to deliver a new bike for me on Christmas Day.

Chapter 9

Date Day

It was Sunday morning. And it sunk in.

I woke up with rumbling nervousness in my tummy, but it wasn't so much about having dinner at Selena's house. The first thought that came to my mind as I opened my eyes was, *What the hell am I going to wear?*

I never had to worry about this kind of thing before because I never went out with anyone, much less on a date, and up until now the tiny collection of clothing that I had was sufficient. I had my usual gym outfit, a couple of pairs of jeans, and a small collection of shirts and T-shirts that I picked up at thrift shops. I started to get a little panicky. How can I go to dinner in an affluent area dressed like a mannequin in a thrift shop window? I jumped out of bed, straight to the wardrobe. Maybe by some miracle, I had a decent shirt in there that I forgotten about. In a state of panic, I started pulling out every item of clothing that was in the wardrobe:

"No…no…not that…this one is gross…maybe this shirt? Damn! It has a hole in it…"

Everything I had was suitable for going out to Remi's corner shop, and nothing suitable to wear to a glamorous dinner. I sat on the bed in a state of despair. I started running options in my head:

"Maybe Josh has something I can borrow?" This idea wouldn't work because he was bigger than me.

"Maybe his sisters!?" I jumped on my feet. "They're in the fashion business! Maybe they have something I could borrow!?"

The percolator buzzed to indicate that the coffee was ready. I love my percolator, it's the only thing that connects me to the hi-tech world. I don't have a cell phone or a computer. Just a percolator that kicks in automatically.

I poured myself some coffee, while still trying to think of ways to get some decent clothes for tonight. It was a bit too early to call Joshua on a Sunday morning, so I decided to wait till mid-morning and then call him. Meanwhile I sat on the bed with my cup of coffee and watched some mind numbing program on TV to pass the time.

Ten o'clock came around, and I hadn't even noticed. I was just slumped on my bed, motionless, staring at the TV screen almost as if I were hypnotised. My head was slightly tilted to the right, and my eyes were barely blinking. I was like a mental patient on tranquilizers. Everything that was coming out of the television was just soaking up

161

into my spongy brain. Suddenly, the doorbell rang and jolted me out of the trance I was in.

"Just a minute!" I shouted and turned down the TV volume.

Who could it be at ten o'clock on a Sunday morning? I wondered. "Better not be Jehovah's Witnesses!" I muttered and walked toward the door.

"Who is it?" I asked.

"Sam, it's Lisa," the voice on the other side of the door yelled.

Lisa is my neighbor down the hall. We both share a wall with Mick and Donna, the fighters from hell, and we often share jokes about their episodes. I unlatched the lock and the chain on the door and opened it quickly.

"Hi, Lisa," I greeted her with cheerful but tired voice.

"Did I wake you?" she asked.

"No, I was just comatose by the TV," I joked.

Lisa laughed. "Yeah, that dreaded mind control apparatus; I avoid it like the plague." She kept laughing and lifted the plastic bag she was holding.

"What's that?" I asked, still with a tired voice.

"I thought maybe you could use this suit," she said. "I bought it for Daniel, but he's all obsessed with the latest trends and thought it was lame and unfashionable, and he doesn't want to wear it. Since you two are the same size body, I thought maybe you could use it, if you're not too fussy that is." She laughed and handed me the bag.

I took the bag and looked inside. There was a complete dinner outfit in there with a jacket and a belt to go with the black pants.

Lisa noticed the look of horror on my face. "Don't you like it?" she asked.

My eyes started to tear up as I looked at Lisa. "Wow, Lisa! You won't believe this, but you've just created a miracle," I said as I gave her a big hug.

"That's okay, Sam. It's only a suit; no need to get emotional," she said, laughing.

No need to get emotional? If she truly knew the full meaning of what her gesture meant, she'd be in tears too.

"Thank you so much!" I gushed. "Thank you so much!"

"You're welcome, Sam. I hope you put it to good use," she said kindly.

"You have no idea!" I said with a chuckle

"Mick and Donna have been very quiet lately. Have I been missing any important episodes?" she asked with a giggle.

I laughed. "I was thinking the same thing." I then leaned over to her and whispered, "Last time, the bacon wasn't crispy enough."

"Oh, I've heard that episode. I guess I'm caught up," she whispered and laughed. "Well, I better be going; I have two hungry boys waiting for their breakfast. I better get their bacon crispy. Enjoy the suit!" she said cheerfully and walked toward her apartment.

"Thanks again, Lisa," I said in a meaningful expression of gratitude and closed the door. I stood there for a minute with the bag in my hand, then looked up and sighed a big thank you.

As I pulled the pieces out of the garment bag, to take a better look at what was inside, I couldn't help thinking about what Gabe told me about everything being provided for us when we're on our path. As much as I would like to have called this a coincidence, it was way too obvious that this was a piece of the puzzle. I mean, what were the chances, of someone knocking on your door with a brand new full suit in a poor neighborhood? I've lived here for three years, and no one ever knocked on my door to offer me anything, and now, right on the day that I needed clothes in order to have a successful evening, Lisa had a complete suit, in the right size, and with a pair of matching shoes.

I spread the content of the bag on the bed. A pair of black pants, a white shirt, a black suit, a black fake leather belt, with a silver rectangular buckle, and a pair of black shoes, in my exact size, made of fake leather and plastic soles.

Amazing! I thought to myself as I looking at the brilliant selection of apparel on my bed. A few hours ago, I was worried, and now, there's a complete suit on my bed, and I didn't even leave the apartment. I must admit, this does feel like a scripted event; it's as if it had been queued up, waiting to be executed at the right time. I would never

164

have imagined something like this happening when I woke up this morning. My mind couldn't come up with any solutions, but the solution came when I let go of trying, and it came with a bang!

My sense of confidence, that tonight's dinner was a significant part of my destiny, got a lot stronger. I was trying hard not to guess the outcome, or make any kind of interpretations beyond that. All I knew was, this was something I needed to do, and it was part of the script in my life's movie, and I felt excited about it.

I dragged myself to the kitchen, leaving the suit spread on the bed, and poured myself another cup of coffee. As I sat at the kitchen table, I took a sip of my coffee and slowly turned my head to look at the clothes on my bed, then I started laughing uncontrollably with joy. I felt like grabbing the Universe and giving it a big heartfelt hug. The emotions I felt translated to laughter, and a feeling of calmness was taking over me. *I'm once again in a joint venture with the Universe,* I thought to myself.

Now it was a waiting game. I thought I'd leave at five o'clock. I needed to take the bus, which was about a forty-five-minute ride outside of Detroit, and pick up a bottle of wine, though I didn't quite know what to get, since I was a teetotaler. I also didn't have much money to buy good wine, but I was sure Remi would know a way around it; he claimed to have the best of the cheapest wines.

I started to get a little nervous as time got closer to five o'clock. I not only hadn't been on a date before, but this wasn't your usual dinner date. It was a dinner date with a daughter of a rich family. It was dinner with Selena's mother and father. Talk about pressure. I now had to be three times as aware, because I'll have an extra two sets of eyes and ears, and if she has siblings, then add more sets to the

165

equation. I started to imagine all of them grilling me over who I was, what I did, where I came from. I saw myself sitting in an inquisition room, where, at the end, the chief inquisitor shouts "Guilty!" or "Not guilty" and slams the gavel.

My heart rate was definitely a little uncomfortable with those images in my head, and to a degree, reduced the level of excitement. Gabe's words again started playing in my head, about how we create scenarios in our minds, that may or may not happen, and we put ourselves in a state of anxiety based on these thoughts.

"I have to keep myself busy," I said to myself. I knew if I were doing something, I wouldn't have time to run scenarios in my head....
"Ahhh!" I said loudly with a tone of excitement as I looked at the TV set. "The master brain sedater!" I said cynically and pushed the on button on the remote. Nothing better than a crappy TV show to numb your brain and stop it from thinking and creating scenarios. I threw myself on the bed, and looked at the clock on the wall.
"four hours to go..." I mumbled and turned toward the screen.

It turned out to be unhelpful. I couldn't even concentrate on the TV. My mind was wandering into all sorts of places. I was looking at the clock every minute, trying to push the time forward with my mind. It was like watching grass grow. After more than two hours of this, I got really uncomfortable. I got up and decided to take a shower and try my new suit on. At least I'd be busy with preparations.

The suit looked amazing. It fit my body exactly. I stood in front of the mirror, just admiring my new suit and my new look. I never wore anything fancier than a pair of jeans and a tee shirt before. I had to stand there and look at myself; I looked like a different person. My short black hair was still a little wet and glistening in the light. My

166

white shirt was buttoned up to the chest and left undone at the top, revealing the top of my muscular chest. I put the black suit on, straightening the creases on its side, and stood straight like a soldier at attention position in front of the mirror, inspecting the final result. I felt a lot more confident and less intimidated, and, to be honest, it actually gave me a healthy boost of self-esteem. I guess "the outside" can be a reflection of "the inside" sometimes. I was so hard on myself all these years and had such low self-worth that I didn't care much for how I looked. Wearing a pair of cheap jeans that hadn't been washed for weeks with the same T-shirt was the norm for me. I had no reason to look good. Who was I going to impress? Looking at it now, the way I dressed was an exact reflection of how I felt inside: neglected and indifferent.

It was time to go. I took one last look in the mirror, while pulling some cool impressions and postures, exhaled sharply, and walked out of the apartment. I was heading over to Remi's to pick up a bottle of his best cheap wine. As I walked out of the apartment building, my landlord was outside, pulling weeds from the side of the building. *This ain't good,* I thought to myself, and kept walking past him. He turned around, looked at me, and said, "Good afternoon, sir." "Good afternoon," I answered back, and I almost fell over.

"Holy crap!" I muttered. "He didn't recognize who I was!" I started chuckling to myself. Maybe I need to wear this suit every time I need to avoid him. He obviously only recognize the scruffy Sam. I laughed and entered Remi's corner shop.

Remi was sitting by the counter looking up at the TV screen that was hanging on the wall, watching a soccer match.

"Good afternoon, boss!" I greeted with a cheery voice.

Remi was still looking up at the screen. He made half a turn toward me and greeted me back, still not realizing it was me. Suddenly, he turned sharply toward me when he realized it was me.

"Holy Bar-B-Q Sunday!" he exclaimed. "Is that you, Sammy boy!? Look at you, maan!" he said excitedly. "I didn't even recognize you!"

I laughed at his reaction, and bowed like a maestro. "I'm going on a date," I said with a tone of excitement.

"Who with? Da queen of England?" he replied with a chuckle.

I laughed and headed over to the wine section, "I need your cheapest best wine."

Remi laughed and shook his head. "You're gonna turn up to a date dressed like royalty, carrying a bottle of cheap wine? Not on my shift, Sammy boy!" he said as he opened a small wooden cabinet underneath the counter and pulled out a bottle of red wine. He dusted off the bottle, gave it a wipe with a kitchen towel, and handed it to me. "This is the kind of wine you need to take," he said.

I took the bottle with a surprised and confused look on my face. "What is this?" I asked still looking confused.

"This is a 1982 multi-vintage Chatto Grange, ma maan; it's one of the best," he said.

"Sounds expensive; I don't know if I can afford it, Remi," I said awkwardly.

"No payment required, ma maan; it's a gift to complement your attire." He laughed.

"Oh, Remi, this is so kind of you," I said delighted. "Thank you very much!" I put my hand in my pocket and took out fifteen dollars. "Here, why don't you take this?" I offered.

Remi started laughing. "If you knew how much this wine was worth, you'd be embarrassed that you've offered me this." he gave me one of his Jamaican handshakes. "Enjoy, me broad."

"Thanks again, Remi. You may have just saved me from a few raised eyebrows." I laughed and walked toward the exit. "I better be going, I still have a long bus ride ahead of me."

"Good luck, Sammy boy; I want to hear all about it."

"Within reason," I said with a cheek. "But that's the least I can do for you in return for your kindness." I chuckled and walked out of the shop.

When I got off the bus, I felt very pleased with myself, as almost every female on the bus tried to get a glimpse of me. Some were more obvious than others. It made me feel attractive and confident to face Selena and her family.

I turned into Selena's street. Every house was like a palace, with big metal gates, and security cameras pointing in different direction. Some properties were so big that it would take a five-minute drive to get to the main house. I started to feel a little intimidated. This is a seriously rich neighborhood. My heart was pounding irregularly as I looked for 44, the number of Selena's house.

"Oh...My...God!" I exclaimed loudly to myself as I stood in front of two big black gates, with the number 44 in the center of the gates. I looked past the gates, still mesmerized by the opulence that was in front of me. There were three cars parked near the house. The road from the gate, led straight to a big open area, with a round fountain in the center. The gardens were impeccably maintained and the color of the flowers in the garden beds surrounding the open area were breathtaking. I stood there for a minute longer, just taking deep breaths, and then I pushed the buzzer on the gate.

"Hello?" a polite voice said through the speaker.

"Hi, it's Sam King. I'm here for Selena," I spoke into the microphone.

"Oh! Hi, Sam! Come on in!" the friendly voice answered, followed with a buzzer sound. I pushed the small side gate open, and walked up the driveway, still looking around and admiring the gardens around the house.

The front door opened as I got closer to the house, and Selena's dad stepped out, and, with a friendly smile, greeted me and shook my hand.

"How are you, Sam? I'm Tony Belzano, Selena's father."

Belzano? I thought to myself. *Where do I know that name from?* I shook his hand firmly. "Nice to meet you, Mr. Belzano."

"Please, call me Tony," he insisted.

"This is for you," I said and handed him the wine.

"Thank you, Sam," he said fondly… "Oh! Chatto Grange!" he said with admiration. "Good choice, Sam!" he put his hand on my shoulder and invited me in.

I smiled to myself, and immediately thought of Remi. It wouldn't have been good if I had handed him a ten-dollar Chatto De Crap, considering the opulence around me. Thanks to Remi, I passed the first hurdle with flying colors.

"Selena is just getting ready; she'll be down in a minute. She knows you're here," he said and led me to the living room.

"No problem," I said softly.

I was a little nervous and a little intimidated to be honest. I'd never hung out with rich people before. I was a little self-conscious and couldn't help feeling overwhelmed. Everything in the house was placed in a precise position and every surface was spotlessly clean. There was a wide spiralling staircase leading to the second floor. The living room was bigger than my whole apartment. Every piece of furniture had an antique flair and shape. Bronze statues were spread around the room. A huge chandelier hung from every ceiling in every room. They looked heavy with various sized crystals hanging from them, glistening in the light. It reminded me of the river at sunset with the sun shining on the ripples, which I always admired.

"Wow!" I said like a child at a magic show. "These chandeliers are huge!" I exclaimed as I looked at the one in the large living room.

Tony laughed. "Yes, they are. We have chandeliers around the place. They weigh between 200 to 500 pounds and are made from pure

171

Lumerian quartz crystals, all shaped and polished individually by hand," he explained, sounding like a tour guide at a museum.

I nodded with a pout, pretending to know what he was talking about, but, in truth, I had no idea what that meant.

"Would you like a drink, Sam?" Tony asked and opened the door to the bar.

"I don't drink alcohol, but I'll have a juice if you have one," I answered.

Tony poured some orange juice into a tall glass and poured himself some whiskey in a shot glass. "I heard what you did for Selena, and I would like to personally thank you for coming to her aid," he said earnestly. "It's not every day that you see a stranger sticking their neck out to help someone in distress," he said and handed me the juice.

"Yeah, I know what you mean," I said sympathetically. "But I was brought up in a family that constantly taught me about the importance of helping others whenever possible, and I'm proud of it." I smiled and took a sip of my juice.

"And so you should be." He smiled and pointed at the couch, suggesting we sit down.

"So what do you do, Sam?" he asked quickly. It didn't take long for him to ask the dreaded question.

"I work for the Detroit advanced disposal team," I said with a smirk. Tony looked at me confused. "A garbage collector," I said straight out and waited for his reaction.

"Oh, nice!" he said.

"Not the most glamorous job, I know, but it's temporary until I find a way to accomplish my ultimate dream," I said with an embarrassed chuckle.

"Nothing wrong with being a garbage collector," Tony replied kindly. "If it weren't for them, we'd be swimming in our own rubbish." He laughed.

"You sound like my colleague, Joshua," I said, laughing. "That's exactly what he says."

"I started my career as a dishwasher slash kitchen hand," he admitted. "Believe it or not, without the kitchen hands, even the most luxurious restaurant would go out of business. We all have to start somewhere, and, for some, it's exactly where they need to be."

I looked at Tony, nodding in agreement. *This guy's down to earth,* I thought to myself. *He doesn't seem like the average rich guy. He even talks like Gabe and Josh.* I always imagined rich people to be condescending and snarly, thinking that they were above those who didn't have as much, and that they were smarter and more important. But Tony debunked all these assumptions in fifteen minutes of conversation.

"So what's your 'ultimate dream,' Sam?" Tony asked curiously.

"My ultimate dream is to open a 'restaurant for the people' and have one in every city," I said with pride and conviction.

"A restaurant for the people?!" Tony exclaimed. "Aren't restaurants already for the people? Well, unless they're 'pet restaurants,'" he joked.

"Not for all people," I replied quickly. "Some people can only dream of affording a meal at a restaurant. I want a restaurant where anyone can afford to eat there, regardless of income or status," I continued explaining.

Tony looked at me, intrigued. He nodded and signaled with his hand for me
to carry on.

"There will be one price for all meals on the menu: ten dollars. I chose that price because that's what I needed to make every day, selling aluminium cans during my homeless days in order to feed myself. Let me tell you, that amount doesn't buy you much healthy food. If they can't afford to pay for the meal, they can donate two hours of their time to either work in the restaurant, washing dishes, cleaning and helping with various tasks in the kitchen, or they can choose to work for one of the charity organizations that will be affiliated with the restaurant. The charity organizations then pay us a small hourly rate for their work in return. This system gives those less fortunate an opportunity to convert their skills and energy into a meal without using money. The charity organization that employs them, usually as gardeners, cleaners, and general maintenance jobs, get a constant stream of helpers at a much lower rate than professionals would charge. This rate will be enough to cover our costs."

I stopped talking after I noticed that Tony's face was straight, and his eyes squinted.

"So, you're saying that ten dollars is going to cover cost?" Tony asked skeptically, as if he had just put his business hat on.

"Because there will only be four main meals on the menu and four entrées, there won't be a need to cook each meal to order. The meals are prepared in advance in large batches. This means we're buying the ingredients a lot cheaper in bulk wholesale and have no wastage. This allows for a quick turnover and will benefit the bottom line because if our margins are low, the more meals we sell, the better. If they work for us part time in exchange for the meal, this means we save on wages and benefits. It's a win-win for all involved. The main thing is, we're closing the gap between the have-nots and the have-yachts," I joked.

Tony laughed. "Hmmm... Interesting." He nodded and took a sip of his whisky.

I was starting to wonder where Selena was when, at that moment, she came down the wide spiral stairs like a princess, gracefully walking down, step by step, slowly and carefully.

"Here's my girl!" Tony announced with pride.

I quickly stood up, unable to say a word. She looked breathtakingly beautiful. She quickly greeted me, and kissed me on each cheek.

"My knight in dirty gloves," she said with a giggle. "Nice to see you."

"You look…amazing," I said, flabbergasted. Her olive skin complexion along with the red dress she was wearing, and the black ribbon pushing her hair back, looked picture perfect. like she just came out of a fashion magazine. I was instantly in love.

"Thank you, Sam!" she replied appreciatively. "You're looking pretty amazing yourself! A far cry from the knight in dirty gloves image," she joked.

"Thank you," I replied and looked into Selena's eyes. Our eyes locked together for a couple of seconds, and I think that in those seconds, I may have experienced the first feeling of true love energy like an electrical current rushing through my body from head to toe. My stomach started fluttering and I felt an intense desire to hold her in my arms. This wasn't the same as what I felt with Selena from Frank's Diner. This was a lot more intense, a lot more real. It immediately struck me that maybe what I felt for Selena the waitress was a mere infatuation that must have resulted from my loneliness and a strong longing for a love partner rather than a soul connection that would eventually develop into a magical love story. My soul knew this, and looking back now, I can see how it made sure we never ended up together.

While our eyes were still locked together, Tony noticed that he had two lovebirds on his hands, and quickly jumped in to cool things off.

"Sam told me about his interesting concept for a restaurant," he said to Selena. He then went on to explain to Selena the concept I had just described to him before she joined us. Tony looked more excited than I was. I stood there watching Tony explain the concept to Selena as if he were giving a presentation to a committee of investors.

176

"Interesting and noble. I really like it!" Selena said with an excited supportive tone. "Right up your alley, Dad," she said, smiling.

"How so?" I asked, intrigued by the remark.

Selena laughed and looked at her dad. "Obviously, you haven't told him what you do," she said with a giggle.

I stood there, looking at her curiously, waiting for some more information.

"My dad is the owner of Belzano's, the chain of upscale Italian restaurants. He knows a thing or two about the restaurant business," she said proudly.

"Tony Belzano! Of course!" I exclaimed. "That's where I know your name from! My dad used to say whenever I was being wasteful. 'I'm not the owner of Belzano's.'"

Selena and Tony laughed.

"And here I am in the house of Tony Belzano. It almost feels like fate."

"Amazing!" Selena exclaimed. "What are the chances of this happening? Maybe it is fate!" she laughed and gave me a look of admiration.

"Only time will tell," Tony said and topped up my orange juice.

"Thank you, Tony," I said as he poured the juice.

The energy in the room felt like I was with my family at Christmas. There was a connection between us all. It was as if we had known each other all our lives, despite me only being there for less than an hour. I was very comfortable and had a sense of elevated excitement. All the opulence around me suddenly didn't matter, and I wasn't noticing it anymore. The minute Selena walked into the room, all my attention turned to her; she was the only opulence I could see.

Tony looked at his watch, and suggested we should move to the dining area.

"I'll let the kitchen know we're ready. I hope you're hungry, Sam," he said.

"I am pretty famished," I said and smiled at Selena. She looked at me with admiring eyes again, smiled, and said, "Let's go eat then!"

As we moved toward the dining area, I really wanted to ask something, but I wasn't sure it was my place to ask it. We were all having a great time, but were we the only ones? I kept wondering, *Where's her mom? Is she going to join us? And does she have any siblings?* It seemed strange that only a father and a daughter would live in such a huge estate. In the end, I couldn't contain myself.

"Isn't Mrs. Belzano joining us?"

Selena looked at her dad with smiling eyes, then turned to me and said, "There's no Mrs. Belzano, but we can talk about it at dinner."

Chapter 10

The Dinner

As we sat at the table, I started to get a little nervous. I didn't know if rich people ate in a particular way. Was I supposed to hold the spoon and fork in a particular way? What about the napkin? I saw on TV how they placed it on their lap. Was that what I was supposed to do? As I sat there watching what Selena would do, the door opened, and a maid pushing a trolley walked in.

"Good evening, everyone!" she said cheerfully.

Everyone said good evening back at the same time. Tony went on to introduce me quickly, "Mina, this is Sam, the gentlemen who chased Selena's mugger and recovered her purse,"

"Nice to meet you, Sam," she replied. "That was a heroic thing you did for Selena; God bless you," she said as she placed a large silver tray on the table, along with smaller bowls containing various salads and dips.

I looked at the food and started salivating. It looked so delicious and beautifully presented. The dishes looked like they were made for a queen. Each bowl was made of expensive-looking porcelain with gold around the rims and the letter B on each of them. The salads and dips were all presented with an artistic flair, and the bread was still steaming, suggesting it just came out of the oven.

"Wow!" I said with amazement. "This looks fabulous!"

"These are some of the dishes we serve at our restaurants," Tony said proudly. "So don't hold back, Sam; dig in," he said cheerfully. He then went on to describe each dish, what it contained, and how it was cooked with great enthusiasm. It was obvious to me that Tony was very passionate about his creations.

"This looks so beautiful, I don't want to ruin it. Does the B stand for Bellissimo?" I asked with a chuckle.

Tony and Selena laughed. "It may as well be," Selena said, still laughing.

"As you can see, Sam, it's a real struggle trying to keep in shape while being a Belzano," Selena joked as she handed me a bowl of salad.

"Well, you've done a pretty good job so far," I complimented.

"Thank you, Sam, but this meal will require a few hours of cardio, so that's the down side." She laughed.

My taste buds were having an independence day celebration in my mouth. I was mindful of being gracious and eating elegantly, but really, all I wanted to do was devour the food, as I was ravenous and each mouthful was tastier than the previous. There were a few moments of silence, as each of us was busy eating. Soft classical music came out of speakers that were embedded in the ceiling. At that moment, I thought I had died and gone to heaven.

"How is it, Sam?" Tony asked, breaking the silence.

"It's really hard to find the right words to describe it, Tony, but I think I'm in heaven," I said and looked at Selena with smiling eyes. Selena looked back at me and smiled. "Well, you have found the right words. That's a good way to describe it." She raised her glass. "Cheers!" We all clinked our glasses.

"So, Sam, you asked about Mrs. Belzano," Selena said.

"I didn't mean to pry," I answered quickly and sheepishly. "I hope I didn't offend you."

"You didn't offend us at all," Tony said empathetically. "It was a legitimate question." He smiled and took a sip of his wine.

"Are your parents still around, Sam?" Tony asked.

"My father died a few years ago, and my mother left us when I was ten. So no, they're not around unfortunately."

Selena looked at her dad with a surprised look, then slowly turned toward me.

"I'm sorry to hear that, Sam," she said compassionately.

"My mother left us when I was ten also," she said. "I guess we share a common theme."

"Wow! That's a bit synchronistic," I said, surprised. "I don't know to this day why she left or where she is. I just remember waking up one day, and she was gone. I don't even know if she's alive," I said sadly.

Selena looked at me with empathetic eyes. "That's terrible, Sam! I'm so sorry to hear that," she said compassionately. "I know from experience what it's like not to have a mother around when you're ten, but at least I knew where my mom was and had constant contact with her. But I can't imagine not knowing where your mom is; it must have been so hard for you."

"That's okay," I replied quickly. "What doesn't kill you makes you stronger, right!?" I said with a chuckle, trying to add humor to the somber mood.

"Unless a train hits you and you'd be crippled and in pain," Tony added his humorous touch, sounding like the Godfather with his Italian accent.

"Why did your mom leave?" I asked.

Selena looked at her father, as if she were asking for permission to tell.

"My mother left us for a rich man after Dad's first business failed. She had this idea that life was too short to waste it on struggles.

Ironically, the man she ran away with went bankrupt, and the man she left became wealthy." She laughed.

"Isn't Karma a wonderful thing?" Tony said, laughing.

I nodded in agreement and smiled. I thought that was one of the best cases of poetic justice I had ever heard.

"That must have been hard on your self-esteem," I said softly to Tony. Considering this was always my biggest fear, that I would be rejected because I didn't have much or because I wasn't not good enough, I felt great empathy for Tony in that moment.

"You mean to have my wife leave me because I failed?" he said with a chuckle. "Maybe at first, but then I believe it's better to know the real motives behind what I thought was true love earlier, rather than later; don't you think?" he said eloquently. "My first business failed because I was making bad investments and decisions due to lack of experience, but also I had a high maintenance wife, which made me focus on making money as quickly as I could, rather than coming into my own in my own time, which was like trying to hurry along your veggie garden because you're hungry. This failure not only taught me that passions and greed don't mix but it also removed the phoney aspects from my life, including my wife and some so-called friends," he said, laughing.

"Yeah, I know what you mean," I replied. "For a long time, I believed that unless you had money, you wouldn't be happy or have the means to be happy, but I soon learned that even rich people have problems, and they can't always 'buy' a solution."

"And now you don't believe that you need money to be happy and fulfilled?" Selena asked with cheek in her voice.

"Not since a special friend opened my eyes," I said softly. "That's why I decided to pursue my passions first, rather than aim to make money doing whatever I think will bring it to me, whether I enjoy it or not. I still don't know how I'm going to do it, but that's another story." I laughed.

"Now, that's the main ingredient for success!" Tony exclaimed. "When I was with Tracy, my wife, I was trying to make money as quickly as I could, as I said, but what I didn't tell you, was that I was trying to make money doing things I didn't like, because although my passion was in cooking, I couldn't see how that was going to make me enough money. So I played the stock market, because everyone was making money on stocks. I played the property market, because everyone was making money on property speculations, but I didn't know much about it, and I hated doing it. I borrowed too much, and lost it all. That made me a very unpleasant man to be around, and Selena can attest to that." He laughed and Selena nodded in agreement with a cheeky grin on her face.

"In a way," Tony continued, "It was a blessing because after Tracy left, I was able to focus on what I love without the pressure of trying to please her and ended up building Belzano's in my own good time. The interesting thing was, I wasn't even aiming to make a lot of money; it just grew over time. The next logical steps just presented themselves, and all I had to do was follow them, and I enjoyed every aspect of it. You see, Sam, having lots of money comes with great responsibility. Most people want money because money is their main concern and worry. They never get to see the other problems that come once you have it, so not everyone has the character to handle lots of money."

"Well, as the old cliché goes, money can't buy you happiness, right!?" I said meaningfully.

"It may be cliché, but it's true!" Tony exclaimed with a chuckle. "Now, do I like having money? Sure! But I also know that with money comes a great responsibility to use it for the greater good. I don't fool myself into thinking that it's the source of my happiness. So, I made a conscious effort to raise my children on values and morals and always encouraged them to follow their heart and do what they love. My son, Tony Jr., decided to pursue a career in sports and Selena wanted to pursue her passion for helping children and become a child psychologist, and both are doing well and are happy." Tony looked at Selena proudly and squeezed her hand gently.

"But to be fair," I said, "having financial security is a huge plus, and everyone wants that. I'm not saying it's everything, but it's definitely nice to have."

"Do you think that someone who has money is secured for life?" Tony asked. "They can just as easily lose it all. Most rich people live with huge debts and are relying on constant income to keep them afloat. They frequently lose sleep worrying about losing it or how to keep it; trust me. You see movie stars and athletes who go broke, despite earning millions. You see billionaire businessmen go broke when shares plummet. The more money they have, the more they're worried about financial security for themselves and their families. They're aware of the possibility of kidnapping and extortions. My kids went to school with bodyguards watching over them the whole time when we lived in Los Angeles, and Selena hated that, didn't you?" Tony looked at Selena and laughed.

"Yes I did!" Selena answered. "I used to wish I was a normal girl in a normal working class family."

"Most people don't see that," Tony continued. "They just see the glitzy side of it on TV or tabloids, and they dream about what they'd do if they had that kind of money. They think that if they had lots of money, they'd just sit back and enjoy spending it. If only they knew." Tony laughed. "Rich people don't want to retire because money isn't the end game when you're enjoying what you're doing. In fact, they end up working till their last days. The truth is, Sam, most people should be secured if they learned to live within their means and start looking in their own backyard to see the hidden treasures in their lives."

I laughed and shook my head.

"Why are you laughing?" Selena asked with a slight giggle.

"I'm laughing because of how synchronous this is. I had this conversation with my friend Joshua a few days ago, and he said the same thing. He called credit a modern-day devil and greed is his cousin."

"I like that!" Tony said with a chuckle. "You only have to look at how many people do jobs they hate because it pays for the things they can't afford to see that it's true. Joshua is a wise man!"

"Yes he is," I said quietly, nodding in agreement.

"Let's drink to that then!" Tony announced and lifted his glass. "Salute!"

"Salute!" we all cheered back, raising our glasses.

Tony took a sip of his wine and slowly lowered the glass to the table with a serious expression on his face. "Having said that, Sam," he exclaimed. "I always believed that those who have acquired wealth have the responsibility of using it for the greater good and to help others. I was looking for an opportunity to do that, and you just gave me one," he said meaningfully and smiled.

"How so?" I asked surprised.

"I think your restaurant concept can give me that opportunity. Not only is it within my area of interest but its altruistic value is second to none, and considering your act of selflessness you showed with Selena, I think it's more than fair. So…. I'm going to help you realize your ultimate dream. I'll fund the first restaurant, and we'll see how that goes before opening others."

"Oh my God!" Selena exclaimed and jumped in her seat. "This is awesome!"

I sat there frozen for a few seconds. I felt an electric charge running through my body from my head town to the pinkie toe. I hoped that I wasn't in a dream from which I was about to wake.

"I don't know what to say, Mr Belzano. I'm dumbfounded….thank you so much!" I said shakily, on the verge of tears.

"Well, it looks like we haven't seen the last of you yet," Selena joked.

187

"You're welcome, Sam," Tony replied. "We'll start drawing the concept and get the ball rolling. There's a lot to do, including finding a suitable venue and fitting it out."

Selena, with a big grin on her face, clasped her hands together and squeezed them with excitement. It almost looked as if she were more excited than I was. I didn't know what I was more excited about: the fact that I was about to fulfil my dream or the fact that I'd get to see Selena more often. Either way, this was a moment I would never forget, the moment I was given a new lease on life.

When dinner was over, we all sat there full and fulfilled. It was a dinner I can't describe with words. I exhaled sharply, suggesting I was full. My stomach was struggling to digest the food, given the churning that was going on in there as a result of the news. I looked at Selena with smiling eyes. She looked so beautiful and radiant, and I was clearly smitten. Selena suddenly came up with the best solution…

"Sam, do you want to go for a walk around the garden? You look like you ate too much."

This couldn't come at a better time, I thought to myself.

"That's exactly what I need to calm the Armageddon that's going on in my stomach right now!" I said enthusiastically.

Tony laughed. "Did you eat too much, Sam? It's a common occurrence with our diners," he teased.

"Yes! I definitely ate too much! But I'm digesting the food and the news with one digestive system. It appears to be in overload." I laughed and stood up, ready to go outside.

"It's a beautiful night," Tony reinforced. "You two go ahead; I have some work to do upstairs." Tony stood up and walked toward the door.

"Thanks again, Tony... for everything," I said, trying to sound as sincere and as appreciative as I could.

"No... thank YOU, Sam!" he said as he walked out of the room.

Did he just thank me? I thought to myself. I looked at Selena with a stunned look on my face. Selena noticed the look, smiled, and nodded. "Yep!" she said, "you sure made an impression on him." She laughed and put her arm around mine.

"Clearly!" I chuckled as we walked outside.

It was a beautiful night. The skies were clear, and we could see the stars quite clearly. Billions of them covering the sky like a blanket of glitter, all different sizes and intensities. The light posts around the garden, were shining a soft light directly onto the garden beds, highlighting the flowers below. The sound of frogs chirping from the ponds in the garden, filled the air. Like a subtle whistle that kept going on and on without a pause. I felt I was on the set of *Alice in Wonderland.* And all that with a beautiful woman in my arms. *Life doesn't get any better,* I thought.

As we stood there, admiring the scene around us, I felt Selena's hand squeezing my arm tightly. She then looked at me....

"I'm so glad that my dad is helping you with the restaurant for the people idea," she said with a soft voice, squeezed my arm again, and gently stroked the top of my hand. Her touch sent tingles through my body, a sensation I hadn't felt before. The butterflies in the stomach feeling. I felt my knees weakening and my heart was pounding at a fast rate. I held her hand, and gently stroked it, feeling the warmth of the inside of her palm.

"I'm still trying to digest it, to be honest," I said softly while holding her hand and rubbing it gently. "The last few weeks have been life changing for me, and, as much as I would love to share it with you, I know you probably won't believe me, and I don't want to risk you thinking I'm a lunatic," I said softly with a slight chuckle.

We started walking slowly down the path to the other side of the garden.
"Sounds intriguing," Selena said her interest piqued. "But I doubt I would think you're a lunatic. Lunatics don't chase muggers and recover purses." She laughed.

"Or maybe they do. Maybe you'd have to be a lunatic to chase a mugger the way I did."

"My knight in dirty gloves," she said, giggling and leaned her head on my shoulder.

We stopped walking. I turned around facing Selena and stoked her hair gently.

"I will be forever grateful to that mugger." I smiled and slowly brought my lips closer to hers, until they touched. As we kissed, I closed my eyes and felt my head slightly spinning. Time stopped. I was in the moment, just feeling Selena's soft lips on mine. It was our first kiss, and the only kiss ever that made me feel a real connection to someone. In that moment, I knew that Selena would be the one I would spend the rest of my life with.

We sat down on a rock by the pond, leaning against a large tree. Selena was sitting close by my side, with her head on my shoulder, as I put my arm around her. The sound of the water fountain in the middle of the pond was almost hypnotizing, and blended in well with the chirping frogs. We just sat there, not saying a word and just listening. I almost felt a sense of weightlessness, and I was most definitely in love.

She stroked my arm gently with her fingers, her head still on my shoulder. She was pushing slightly, trying to get as closer as she could to me, as I was holding her tight. We were one, entangled together, letting the love energy that was flowing between us engulf us both. She slowly lifted her head, and gazed up at me with the sweetest innocent look.

"Well?" she said with a cheeky tone.

"Well what?" I answered with a slight chuckle.

"Are you going to tell me your life-changing story?" she held my hand and kissed it, trying to entice me, and it worked. At that moment, I could give her the world on a silver platter, which was much more than my life-changing story.

"Are you sure you're ready for this? I mean, it's not your usual life-changing story. It would probably be classified as delusional by most people," I said with a hint of warning in my voice.

Selena chuckled. "But I'm not 'most people.'"

"No, you're not," I agreed. "Okay then... You asked for it!" I said tentatively and exhaled sharply, feeling a little nervous.

I leaned back on the tree. Selena leaned against me, with her head on my chest. I put my arm around her, and held her close to my heart. We sat there for hours, as I told her everything. How my mother left, how my father died. I told her about my rock bottom moments, and how I met Gabe at a time when I was ready to put an end to my miserable life. I told her about Joshua and his story with Nathaniel. I told her about my infatuation with the other Selena. I even told her about the suit, and how I got it. Selena just sat there listening, not saying a word.

"And that's how I met you and your father," I ended the story.

Selena, after a long pause, exclaimed, "Wow!"

"I know, crazy, right? I said nervously.

"It's crazy and it's beautiful," she said empathetically. "And I believe everything you told me. I'm blown away, but I believe it," she said with a giggle.

192

"Phew!.. You have no idea how relieved I am that you didn't ask me to leave," I sighed.

Selena laughed. "I mean, it's an out-there story, but I truly believe what Gabe told you to be true. I always sensed that there was more to us than just wake up, go to work, pay bills, and die. I myself, have always felt that we're guided, I always knew that we have a purpose beyond the mundane life we're living, and I have a few stories of my own. I haven't met a Beggar, but I sure did have a lot of synchronicities, and I did think of them as good luck of some sort. Your story just reinforced to me that it wasn't just luck. Even as you were telling me the story, I was thinking back on things that happened, and they all meet somewhere, just as Gabe told you they would. They make sense now when I think back on them. I think I'm going to sit in the canoe and let the stream carry me."

I asked, "Is there room for two?"

"Most definitely!" she exclaimed with a chuckle. "Are you proposing?"

I looked back at her, gently pulled her toward me, and held her tight. "I don't mean to get ahead of myself," I said softly while holding her as close to me as I could. "But I could easily fall in love with you."

Selena smiled, and looked at me with sparkling eyes. "You're not ahead of yourself, Sam. I liked you the moment I saw you with or without your dirty gloves. I could easily fall in love with you also. I feel I'm exactly where I need to be right now."

"Me too," I said quietly. "There's no other place I'd rather be right now."

193

Selena put her head on my chest and whispered, "Thank you, Gabe for saving Sam's life."

Chapter 11

The Grand Opening

After that magical night at Selena's house, I was very busy for three months. We managed to find a good venue for the restaurant. It was spacious enough to accommodate a large number of diners, and in a good location. The carpenters were working around the clock fitting the place out according to the design that Selena and I drew. We were one week from the scheduled opening and everything was moving at a fast pace. Every day, a large parcel would arrive containing some piece of the interior: fridges, benches, tables, chairs, ovens, cook tops, and the like. It was like the longest Christmas ever. Every time a delivery arrived, I'd be opening the box with so much excitement, wondering what it was. At times, I would just stand there and watch the carpenters at work. I would listen to the continuous noise of the saws and hammers, and watch the pieces being put together. Sometimes, I would pinch myself to make sure I wasn't dreaming and that it was really happening. My restaurant had materialized.

A lot happened to me in the past three months. I moved out of my derelict apartment after Tony agreed to pay me a wage, since I couldn't continue with the garbage-collecting job, as I needed to oversee the development of the restaurant, and this was a full time job. I found a small apartment in a more modern and quieter area outside of Detroit, but close enough to the restaurant so I didn't have to rely on public transport, or a car, which I didn't have. Nonetheless, it was refreshing to not have to anticipate a knock from my landlord, demanding his rent, or listening to another episode of *Days of Our Lives* staring Mick and Donna. I even bought a cell phone and computer and joined the high tech club. It's a bit strange sometimes when the phone rings in my pocket. At times, I feel like a converted Amish with the way I'm bumbling with the phone apps. But I'm slowly getting used to it.

Leaving the garbage collection job, however, wasn't easy. I obviously missed Joshua, and, in a strange kind of way, I missed that routine. I guess I'm looking back at it from my new milestone, which gave me a different view to the one I had when I was in it, and, from that point of view, I missed the shouting conversations with Joshua and the fun of riding on the back of the truck. My last day there was very emotional, saying goodbye to everyone, and, in particular, Joshua. Of course, Joshua understood the meaning of life's transitions, and although he said that he was sad to see me go, and that his shift would never be the same again, he was the first to bless me for reaching my next milestone. Joshua said that he tends not to jump to conclusions regarding the meaning of signs and synchronicities, but for what it's worth, he thought that when I met Selena, the garbage job had served its purpose. Maybe he's right, but, obviously, he had forgotten the impact that meeting him had on my life. Whichever way the interpretation goes, one thing is for certain, this garbage job was

196

clearly an important segment in my life, and I shall forever be grateful for this time of my life. As Gabe said, hindsight is the best interpretation to the signs and synchronicities along our path.

My relationship with Selena got stronger and tighter in the last three months also. We both felt that we were made for each other, and every day, we thank each other for being there. It was a kind of a ritual we adopted as a reminder that neither of us was taking the other for granted.

Selena continued to work as a child psychologist, and still conducted therapy meetings, but the rest of the time, she spent helping me with the restaurant. That was the only time we got to spend together. I started at six in the morning, and didn't get home before ten o'clock at night, seven days a week. We talked about moving in together at some point once everything settled with the restaurant, and we got some form of normality back. For now, we were both happy to sacrifice our comfort for the greater good.

Unfortunately, this crazy schedule would continue until next week's opening. We were in a race against time with a week to go and nowhere near ready. Everyone was stretched to their maximum capacity. The press releases were already out, and the news media was already prepared to do a cover story on the restaurant. So, we had to finish everything by the due date, and the pressure was at full force on everyone. Despite the stress and the pressure, there was an underlying sense of excitement in me that managed to diminish the anxiety and pressure this venture was causing me. I had never felt so eager to get out of bed in the morning. It was a far cry from the days when I used to drag myself out of bed, feeling depressed and run down. I had a sense of purpose now, felt that I was doing what I was put on this good Earth to do, and I was enjoying it immensely. Adding to that, I was in a relationship with an amazing woman. Sometimes, I couldn't believe how lucky I was to have met Selena. The most amazing part about this relationship is that we were brought together supposedly by a mere chance, a mere coincidence, two people seemingly at the right place and time. But it was obvious to me that we were destined to meet. What would have happened if I had pursued Selena at Frank's Diner? Would I have changed my destiny? I often think about that, and I often look back and see how something I was so upset about turned out to be such a blessing. Now this is a good hindsight interpretation. It made me think of how Joshua met his wife right after missing a bus and possibly losing a job.

I admit that I can't help trying to analyze and study the language of the Universe. I have enough faith in me right now to accept it if my analysis is wrong and to trust that the Universe has my back, even when I guess it wrong. But I also enjoy recording the steps that were prepared for me, because it's so clever. It can be mind-blowing at times when you think about them.

The chain of events leading to meeting Selena were absolutely ingenious. First, it was the infatuation with Selena at Frank's Diner. Then the strange "coincidence" when Remi flirted with his friend Selena. Then I find out that waitress Selena left town, which made me oversleep and late for work, which changed the time we were supposed to finish the run, and I can't help but conclude that it was to align the timing with Selena's, because had I not been late, we would have finished that section way before Selena was mugged. When I look back at the pieces that completed this beautiful picture, it's quite obvious to me now that I was predestined to meet her. It seemed as though the steps were already in the ethers waiting to be executed in their appointed timing, in order to help me unravel this chapter of my life.

Everything that happened around Selena at Frank's Diner was to heighten my sensitivity to the name Selena, which would have been required when I met my Selena, because when she said her name, it made such an impact on me, that it overpowered my insecurities and fear of dating woman because I was poor, working in garbage, and living in downtown Detroit. When she said her name, I was already prepared to see it as significant, and not reject her dinner invitation, despite the fact that I was in my dirty work clothes, and she was in her trendy work clothes. Without those steps, I would have definitely been intimidated by her, and probably reject her dinner invitation. My soul made sure that I wouldn't be and prepared me for that moment. Amazing architecture.

As time got closer to the opening day, my excitement was off the chart, along with growing nervousness. The write up about the opening was coming out in today's paper, forcing me to wait with great anticipation for the paper delivery. The place started to look like a restaurant, and we were in the last stages of cleaning, and final detailing. Tomorrow was the opening, and we were expecting lots of guests, mainly from Selena's side. Being Italian, she had an extended family and friends, and that was enough to fill up the venue. As far as *my* guests were concerned, well, I invited Joshua and his family, Lisa, my former neighbor in downtown Detroit, who gave me the suit, and Remi, who gave me the expensive bottle of wine for my first date with Selena. I guess I still don't have much of a circle of friends, and right now, I was happy just being with my best friend, Selena. It would be nice to see Josh too. I haven't seen him since my farewell from the depot, and with all that's been going on, I didn't have time to keep in touch with him. I missed him. He had been a huge part of my life; he was the one who kept me from going insane, and without him, I would have been lost inside a mental maze. He was my anchor, and I wanted him to be proud of what I've achieved. Sam King, the restaurateur.

Tonight, Selena and I, are going out to dinner to celebrate tomorrow's opening. We were both excited and nervous and needed some time to unwind and catch our breath. Tony booked us a table at one of his restaurants, so we were sure to be treated like a king and queen; no pun intended.

THE OPENING DAY.

Everyone was expected to arrive around midday. The chefs that Tony organized, started prepping the catering at eight in the morning. In order to showcase our menu, we were offering all the dishes we served in a buffet style. The cocktail waitresses were ready with trays of champagne, and a three-piece jazz band would be playing in the corner, courtesy of Tony Belzano, who is a jazz fan. The place looked immaculate with hand-painted art on the walls, soft yellowish light throughout the place, and candelabras with burning candles hanging on each post. If you didn't know, you'd think that this was another one of Tony's restaurants, and not a restaurant for the common people. But this was exactly how I wanted it. I wanted the not-so-fortunate people to experience the look and feel of a trendy restaurant, but without the need to rob a bank in order to pay for the meal. Whether you were rich or poor, the motto of the restaurant was, 'We're all equal, we're all one.'"

The guests started arriving one by one. Selena and I were standing by the front entrance ready to meet and greet the guests. It was also a good opportunity to meet the rest of Selena's family, which made it easier, considering the size of her family. They all came in with their wives by their side, each wearing their own unique colorful outfit, and with loud, heavy Italian accents. Selena went on to introduce me to them, which soon overloaded the name memory capacity of my brain.

The place was buzzing with the sound of soft jazz music wafting across the room, mixed with loud indistinct chatters. The cocktail waitresses were bestowing heart-stopping smiles, while manoeuvring around the guests with trays full of champagne glasses and finger foods. Media photographers were snapping photos of guests, and anything they bumped into along their way. It looked like a Hollywood event made for celebrities.

I stood there, just watching everyone having a good time. One by one, they came up to me to congratulate me, and comment on how beautiful the place looked, and how tasty the food was. Lisa came and complimented me on how good I looked in my suit. Remi came and talked the band into playing some Reggae music. But something was still missing. Joshua. I kept looking out for him, hoping that he'd show up, when suddenly, a hand tapped on my shoulder. I turned around, and there he was with Louisa by his side.

"Now the party is complete," I said with a tone of elation and gave him a big bear hug and kissed Louisa on the cheek.

"It's nice to see your life unfolding, Sam. This place looks amazing! Well done!" he said excitedly and handed me a small box containing the wooden figurine of a beggar.

"Here," he said, "I made this one especially for you. I'm sure you'd be able to relate." He laughed.

"Wow!" I said, choking with emotion. "This is amazing!"

This wasn't just a beautifully crafted piece; it had a special meaning that only Josh and I could relate to, and it made me a little emotional. On closer inspection, I saw that the figurine had a huge resemblance to Gabe.

"This looks exactly like Gabe," I said with amazement. "How—"

Josh quickly responded, "I just let my mind lead my hands, and this is what came out," he said. We both laughed and hugged each other.

"Come on in," I invited cheerfully. "Let me introduce you to Selena and all her relatives."

Now that Josh was here, the picture was complete, and the only thing left for me to do was to soak up the atmosphere and mingle with the guests.

Everyone was in a great mood, drinking and laughing. Some even decided to dance to the jazz band, despite the slow and monotonous beat. I guess when the champagne is flowing, even a jazz band is sufficient for dancing. Josh, Louisa, and Selena hit it off immediately. Selena remembered Josh from the day she was mugged, and a few jokes about it were made between them, at my expense, of course. But watching it from the sideline, it was a heart-warming view to see the most precious people in my life, Josh and Selena, getting on so well.

As the party was nearing the end, and all the speeches were given, the place looked like a hurricane just whizzed through it. The buffet was demolished to its last crumb, and all the champagne bottles were empty. Even I had a few glasses. For someone who doesn't drink, that can wreak havoc on the head and body, and it did.

I walked outside to breathe some fresh air. It was nice and cool outside. The sun started to set, leaving a sliver of golden light in the sky. My head was down, and I was trying really hard not to throw up on the sidewalk. I felt a slight dizziness and a strange ringing in my ears. Trying to control it, I lifted my head up, and on the other side of the road, there he was. Gabe was standing there, looking right at me. He smiled, lifted his hand slowly, and waved. His deep blue eyes were glistening in the twilight, and my eyes were wide open like a child in complete awe. I looked directly at him and felt the same calmness that engulfed me when I first met him. I smiled back and lifted my hand slowly, waving back at him. "I did it," I whispered to him. I felt emotional, tears started to well up in my eyes, and my heart filled with a feeling of love and gratitude. I had this sense that thank you wasn't enough, that no matter what I did or said to try to express how grateful I really was, it just didn't feel enough.

Selena noticed what I was doing and came outside. I was still standing there with my hand up, but she couldn't see anyone in the direction I was waving.

"Who are you waving at, baby?" she asked with a slightly slurred speech.

I looked at her with smiling eyes that were still glistening from the tears and ran my hand along her hair.

"It's Gabe, isn't it?" she said after noticing the emotional expression on my face. I nodded gently in confirmation and pulled her close to me.

"Is he there now?" she asked.

Gabe looked at me, still smiling, and mimed rowing motions at me before he vanished. I understood immediately what he was saying to me, it was a gesture suggesting sitting in a canoe and letting the flow of life carry you. I smiled, looked at Selena, and shook my head gently.

"No, he's not. He's gone." I put my arm around Selena. "Come on; let's get back inside," I said softly and led her into the restaurant.

This was definitely the highlight of the day for me. I didn't expect to see Gabe again, much less him witnessing my next milestone. Despite Joshua revealing to me that I saw Gabe with my mind's eye, to me, he was as real to me as Selena. I couldn't help developing an affinity for him, the same way I would with any human who cared for me that much unconditionally. I wanted to hold onto the notion that he was a real person who did something incredible for me, someone I owed my life to. That was how I intend to keep it.

I know that it's possible that I'll never see him again, but I'll forever remember everything that he told me. I'm quite happy to sit in the canoe and be led by the flow. To be honest, sitting in the canoe right now seemed like the best thing for me to do. Tomorrow we opened for business, and I couldn't help feeling nervous and a little apprehensive. The opening party was over, and now it was crunch time. I remember Gabe telling me that when I'm on my path, things work out effortlessly, and I'm fully supported when I'm where I need to be. This was exactly the kind of mindset that I needed right now, and I was going to trust that whatever happens will be exactly what's supposed to happen, and, so far, it's been an amazing ride.

At times, I would think that maybe Gabe put some kind of a magic spell on my life, and made it the way it was now. I think back at the time when I felt that suicide was easier than living, feeling debilitated by the depressions and anxieties, living in the midst of mortal coil, and I can't help wondering why my life changed so dramatically after my conversations with Gabe. Would I still be alive today had he not showed up when he did? I'm not entirely sure, but I do understand now, that Gabe was simply my guide and not a wizard. He didn't have a magic wand that favored me, that created miracles just for me. I'm sure that everything that happened in the past few months would have happened regardless of whether Gabe showed himself, or not. But the only thing is, I'm not sure I was prepared to wait for it. I was heading for the exit.

Gabe didn't create my path; he was my GPS to my destiny. All he did was make me aware that there's a structure and order to the universe, and, for each soul on this planet, there's a purpose. There's no such thing as randomness. He taught me that this Universe operates in a precise manner with no coincidences and no luck. He made me aware, that each of us was given a mission at birth to complete, and we have all the tools we need to get there. We're not alone on this journey. Our lives are meaningful beyond the mundane tasks that we perform and live through in our daily lives, and the trick to a happier life is to trust that all the pieces will come together in their due time.

Gabe showed himself to me at a time when I was at a breaking point but also a stone's throw from the next turn. Gabe gave me the drive to push along just a tiny bit more because he knew that I was about to do something very silly just before a big turning point in my life that I could never see or even believed was possible.
This made me think about all those people who give up on life like I did just before they reach the turning point to the next milestone

because they can't see it and don't trust that life will reveal the next turn in its due time. I get that now, and I can see what Gabe meant when he said that most people judge the flavor of the cake by tasting the individual ingredients, rather than tasting it once all the ingredients were combined, and the baking process was finished. Such a clever metaphor.

He gave me the ability to understand that life speaks to me, and what it means to live. In the human body, every single organ and cell is there for a particular reason and must accomplish its purpose precisely in order for the body to remain functioning the way it supposed to and stay healthy. If a cell goes rogue, it creates cancer, and if a soul goes rogue, it creates discords and disharmony. The more aware I get, the more I notice how many people are lost along their path, trying to live someone else's path, trying to accomplish what they weren't meant to accomplish in their life. Going in the wrong direction, rowing upstream.

I now see what Gabe meant when he said we were brainwashed to be unaware of our true selves. From the time we were born, we're led astray, away from our purpose and who we really are, and into a competitive and shallow world of ego. We then spend the rest of our lives, trying to accumulate material possessions, and work hard to create an image of ourselves in order to fit into the ego realm. This was the main trap for me and the main cause of my anxieties and depressions. My soul was constantly playing a tug of war with my ego, and, let me tell you, this wasn't a very pleasant feeling. I much prefer the method of "trust, and be led" as oppose to trying to create a life that wasn't designed for me.

I've never been happier, and this feeling of happiness is so new to me. It feels as though I've discovered a human emotion that I didn't know existed and had no idea what it felt like, until now. I'm in a loving relationship, and doing what I love to do. I live modestly but feel that it's adequate, and I have no desire for more. My life now is the result of my past experiences. Everything that I had been through was for the purpose of getting me to where I am now. Before, I was judging my life and constantly condemning it. I can now see that most of my unhappiness and depression was caused by trying to take control and redirect the river in a different direction to the one it was flowing. Trying to achieve what my ego thought I should achieve and constantly going against the path that I was meant to go down, I was stuck in the middle of a tug of war between my soul and my ego. I now understand that I'm not here to create a life from scratch and be the main architect of it. I'm here to unravel the path that was designed for me and experience the different milestones that were put along my path. This is a life lesson I'll always follow, whether things are falling apart or coming together.

A lesson given to me by my guide, Gabe, the Beggar.

..........THE END..........

Made in the USA
Las Vegas, NV
27 November 2021

35418333R00122